Fast Women

Fast Women

John Bullock

ROBSON BOOKS

First published in Great Britain in 2002 by Robson Books,
64 Brewery Road, London N7 9NY

A member of the Chrysalis Book Group plc

Copyright © 2002 John Bullock

The right of John Bullock to be identified as author of this work has
been asserted by him in accordance with the Copyright, Designs and
Patents Act 1988

British Library Cataloguing in Publication Data
A catalogue record for this title is available from the British Library

ISBN 1 86105 488 2

Typeset in Times by SX Composing DTP, Essex.
Printed in Great Britain by Mackays of Chatham, Kent

Contents

Dedication

This book is dedicated to those fast women whose courage, determination and skill brought them success and recognition in a sport dominated by men, and the women of today who are hoping to emulate them.

Acknowledgements

I am indebted to the Brooklands Museum Library and the Brooklands Museum Trust for the considerable help they gave me in the research for this book, and particularly to John Granger for painstakingly checking facts and providing additional information about people and events. Also to Bill Boddy, who has done so much to keep the spirit of Brooklands alive.

– John Bullock

Introduction

Ever since men began racing motor cars more than a hundred years ago, women have wanted to do the same, but in order to do so they had to fight prejudice and bias in a sport dominated by men. The men made the rules to suit themselves and the women were expected to accept them.

This was even more so in Britain, where for many years women drivers had to face claims that they would spoil the macho image of the sport; that they would be unable to handle powerful cars safely at speed; that they had neither the stamina nor the physique to withstand the rigours imposed on drivers during races; or that they would be a danger to themselves and to other drivers if they were allowed to take part.

Even when the first purpose-built motor-racing track in the world was opened in Britain, women were banned from racing there, and, when the rules were relaxed to allow them to do so, it was nearly twenty years before the racecourse authorities would allow them to race against men.

Overcoming such prejudice – with the odds stacked so heavily against them – demanded a special breed of women, who not only refused to take no for an answer, but who set about proving their critics wrong by winning races, breaking records and becoming members of successful international works teams.

They showed that beneath the glamour lay a steely determination to succeed and to prove they were not only capable of competing on level terms in every type of event, but that given the right opportunities they could also be winners.

Fast Women is the story of these women and of courage, some of whose remarkable achievements on land and sea and in the air found their way into the record books. They all managed to bring additional glamour and excitement to a sport that has always favoured the brave and the talented, but still has little time for the faint-hearted.

Foreword by Sir Stirling Moss, OBE

The better women racing drivers have never received the credit they deserved for their hard fought battle to be allowed to race on equal terms with the men and some of their outstanding achievements since then. *Fast Women* is a long overdue reminder of their remarkable performances at circuits like Brooklands, Donington Park and Montlhery, near Paris, as well as in races like Le Mans and the Mille Miglia, and their victories in international rallies since the war.

I have always been aware of the determination and skill shown by them because of my mother's own achievements and those of my sister Pat, but John Bullock's well researched and very interesting new book also describes the colourful lives led by many of the famous women drivers, as well as their remarkable performances during a particularly exciting period in the development of the motor car.

Several of the fast women featured in the book became friends of mine after the war, including the brave and attractive Kay Petre, who lapped the notoriously bumpy Brooklands circuit at nearly 135 mph in a massive 10½ litre Delage more than 60 years ago to win the title of the fastest woman driver in Europe.

Her exploits, along with all the other women of skill and courage who are written about so entertainingly, makes *Fast Women* a book that having started reading I didn't want to put down.

1

The Legendary Camille du Gast

At a time when Britain was still in the grip of a twelve-mile-an-hour speed limit, a battle was taking place on the Continent as to who could build the fastest cars and who could win races with them. Speed was also a major factor in America, and it was a wealthy American, William K Vanderbilt Jr, who had the distinction of not only owning the world's fastest car, which was capable of travelling at a mile a minute, but also of being the first motorist to be fined for furious driving.

The cars being raced in Europe, however, were mostly big and heavy, with poor brakes, suspension and steering, and they were difficult to control. But that didn't deter the noted French beauty Camille du Gast, a fearless horsewoman and talent pianist, whose love of speed and disregard for danger were to make her famous throughout Europe. In 1895, when a rudimentary parachute was being developed for use by French balloon crews, she got hold of one and persuaded Señor Capazza, the distinguished aeronaut, to take her two thousand feet up in his hot-air balloon and let her jump from the basket with the parachute strapped to her chest. Fortunately, the parachute opened in time and she landed safely with only a few bruises to become the first woman to make a parachute jump.

Camille du Gast was always fiercely competitive in everything she did and, when the great 687-mile race from Paris to Berlin took place in 1901, she entered her 20hp Panhard; but, because she was the only woman and her car was only half the horsepower of the other 122 taking part, the organisers made her start last. Even so, she finished in 33rd place. But Camille was annoyed at not being able to compete on level terms with the men, and for the 1903 race from Paris to Madrid she purchased one of the fastest racers of the day – an eighty-mile-an-hour De Dietrich, identical to the cars entered by the successful De Dietrich team. Her new car was easily recognisable by its familiar tapering bonnet, characteristic radiator tubes and the spare wheels strapped to the tail.

Fortunately, Camille's husband was a wealthy Parisian businessman, who was able and willing to buy her any car she wanted, and the De Dietrich racing cars were already well-known for their speed and reliability. For her travelling mechanic she chose a man who was not only fearless and understood the intricacies of the car's powerful engine, but was also strong enough to change a wheel quickly every time the many potholes and flints took their toll on the tyres, which happened frequently.

It was a bright and sunny morning on 24 May 1903, when the 207 competitors made their way to the start in Paris. A large crowd of onlookers were there to see them off and, as people gathered round the cars trying to recognise the drivers, few realised that one of them was a woman. Camille's long hair was tucked away beneath her smart motoring hat and a long leather driving coat hid her shapely figure. Her striking green eyes were also hidden behind a large pair of goggles. When the starter's flag fell, the competitors headed out of the city in a large trail of dust, making their way to Tours, the town situated on the road from Paris to Bordeaux, where the Route Nationale crossed the picturesque Loire and which was their first official stopping place.

Since early morning thousands of cyclists had been converging on the town, along with a steady stream of horse-drawn vehicles and the occasional ox wagon and motor-car, their occupants determined not to miss seeing the main sporting event of the year. Flags and bunting hung from the town's buildings, many of which were also bedecked with flowers. Everyone seemed in a festive mood and by midday all the cafés, bars and restaurants were doing a roaring trade.

On the outskirts of the town, at the point where the main road from Paris and Vendome entered Tours, a group of serious-looking officials were carefully checking their timing equipment, while others kept glancing at their watches and scanning the horizon for the telltale cloud of dust that would herald the arrival of the first competitor. They didn't have long to wait, and, as the dust cloud grew larger, they could make out the shape of a car travelling at high speed, swaying violently from side to side as it negotiated each bend in the road.

The spectators lining the route, who had stepped into the road to get a better view, made frantic attempts to get back on to the pavement as the vehicle bore down on them; but, although the mechanic – a small, wiry man, sporting a large moustache and wearing his cap back to front – was blowing the car's rather asthmatic-sounding brass horn for all he was worth, it made little difference. The pavement was by then several deep with late arrivals, who either couldn't or wouldn't give way, leaving the people in the road with nowhere else to go.

Miraculously, the car missed them all, but crowd control had been a problem all along the route from Paris and was to become steadily worse as the race progressed and the number of spectators increased. Many of the thousands who had gone to watch had never seen a racing car before and were taken by surprise at the speeds involved, so much so that several were later killed or injured when they stepped into the road to get a better view and were unable to get out of the way in time.

The leading car was covered in a thick blanket of dust by the time it slid to a halt alongside the official's table at Tours, but it was still possible to distinguish the number 3 painted on the bonnet, and, when the driver removed his goggles and the rather curious close-fitting white cap with large ear flaps – which covered most of his head – the crowd recognised Louis Renault, the pioneer car maker. Louis and his brothers Marcel and Fernand were all taking part in the race, and Renault was the leading car manufacturer in France.

Louis acknowledged the cheers of the crowd, before shaking hands with all the officials and checking that his time of arrival was correct. Then, after taking several long swigs from one of the bottles of wine that had been placed on a side table for the benefit of competitors, he gave another wave to the spectators, climbed back into his car and drove off down the road behind one of the official cyclists, whose job it was to guide competitors through the crowded streets to the other side of Tours, where another group of officials were waiting to record their time of departure.

As soon as Louis Renault had driven off, a large Mercedes arrived at control driven by a burly German called Werner, who with his mechanic was later to have a narrow escape when their car's rear axle broke while they were driving flat out along a fast stretch of road. The Mercedes was closely followed into the Tours control by three of the fierce-looking De Dietrich entries, two of which were driven by Englishmen, Charles Jarrott and a Yorkshireman called Stead; but the third was driven by Camille du Gast. She was already among the race leaders and ahead of several of the more fancied drivers, despite having to cope with road conditions that made overtaking dangerous.

Apart from spectators straying on to the route, the main problem for all the competitors was the large cloud of dust that followed in the wake of each car. Drivers wanting to pass had difficulty seeing the road ahead and in judging distances correctly. Some who were blinded by the dust didn't see the approaching corner and went straight on into the crowd.

The most hazardous stage of the race occurred on the road to Bordeaux, where it passed through Chatellerault, Poitiers and Angouleme, and several well-known drivers were killed or injured there. One car overturned and burst into flames while overtaking at the approach to a level crossing, killing the mechanic; another's steering broke and it left the road and crashed into a tree, killing both occupants; one of the big Mors collided with a Darracq when the driver was blinded by a cloud of dust and both cars were wrecked, then soon afterwards a large Brouhot spun off the road and went into the crowd when the driver swerved to avoid a child.

Marcel Renault was killed trying to overtake a Decauville and his death led to the withdrawal of all the Renault team apart from Louis, who didn't learn about his brother's death until later. The carnage didn't end there. Lorraine Barrow, the veteran of the De Dietrich team, tried to avoid a frightened dog and both he and his mechanic were killed when their car hit a tree at 80 m.p.h. Then Stead, another member of the team, was attempting to overtake Saleron's Mors when both cars collided and the De Dietrich careered off the road out of control and overturned in a ditch, killing the mechanic outright and pinning Stead beneath the steering wheel badly injured.

Camille du Gast saw what had happened and stopped to help, even though she knew that doing so probably meant throwing away any chance she had of victory. Her burly mechanic, helped by some of the spectators, lifted the wrecked car sufficiently for her to crawl underneath into the ditch and give the injured driver first aid, then make him as comfortable as possible until the ambulance arrived. Doctors at the hospital said later that her prompt action probably saved Stead's life.

After rejoining the race, Camille, according to her mechanic, drove even faster than before and seemed unperturbed by the wrecked cars that littered the roadside. Her efforts to overtake the leaders were of no avail, however, because by the time she reached Bordeaux the French government had given instructions for the race to be stopped to prevent any further carnage. The officials not only refused to allow the remaining cars to be driven any further, but insisted on them being towed rather ignominiously to Bordeaux station by teams of horses, to be taken back to Paris by train.

The tragic circumstances that caused the abandonment had far-reaching repercussions and ensured that it was the last capital-to-capital road race to be held in Europe. Even now, 23 May 1903 is regarded as one of motor racing's blackest days, but before the race was stopped Camille did at least show that a woman could compete on equal terms with the men, and her exploits were reported extensively in newspapers and magazines throughout Europe. Apart from the help she gave to Stead, the way in which Camille had battled against dust, stones and the poor road conditions for more than 340 miles, driving at speeds of up to 80 m.p.h., and how she was one of the few drivers to reach Bordeaux unscathed.

With usually only one major race each year, a driver could achieve fame in quite a short space of time. Camille also had the added advantage of being very beautiful and having a vivacious personality, which made her even more popular. Everything she did was widely reported and she became a role model for all the women who craved excitement and wanted to live a more challenging life.

Like many other drivers, however, she lost interest in motor racing after capital-to-capital road races were replaced by rather less exciting events. Much of the glamour seemed to have gone out of the sport and she decided that racing motor boats fitted with high-powered racing-car engines would be a greater challenge and far more exciting. The sport was certainly just as dangerous, because the boats' hulls were not designed to withstand the heavy buffeting they received when travelling at speed through the water, and many disintegrated and sank during races. It was only when leading car makers teamed up with some of the more experienced hull designers that faster and sturdier boats were built, which would not break up and sink so easily.

In 1905 a race across the Mediterranean from Algiers to Toulon attracted a large entry from several countries. It was the most ambitious event to be held since speedboat racing became popular and Madame du Gast had entered her new boat, which was aptly named *Camille*. Immaculately dressed as usual in her light-coloured oilskins, spotless white gloves and familiar yachting cap with gold braid on the peak, which she wore at a jaunty angle, she was one of the first away, but, soon after the last of the competitors had left Algiers, the wind increased rapidly in strength until it reached gale force.

Even the latest design of racing boats, because of their very low freeboards and open cockpits, couldn't cope with such appalling conditions and many of them were in serious trouble long before halfway. Several sank and their crews were dragged from the water and taken on board either the naval torpedo boat doing escort duty or one of the many small fishing boats running for shelter. Several competitors tried to turn their boats round and return to Algiers, but the high seas made doing so very difficult; and, to add to all the other problems, many of the crew members were violently seasick.

As the few remaining competitors neared Toulon the weather seemed to get even worse and Camille and her crew kept their boat afloat only by frantically bailing with anything they could find every time a large wave crashed down on to them. They managed to keep going towards the finish, despite the sea water that kept finding its way into the carburetter intake and stopping the engine. Every time that happened the carburetter had to be stripped down and cleaned before the engine could be restarted and they could get going again.

In spite of all the efforts of the crew, the boat was taking on board so much water that there was little hope of their reaching land, then suddenly the cruiser *Kleber* appeared out of the mist. Even then their troubles weren't over. The ship was rolling so badly in the gigantic seas that, after trying for two hours to come alongside and pass a rope across to the stricken boat, Commander Paupie, the cruiser's very experienced captain, decided that the only way to save Camille and her crew would be to lower one of the cruiser's own lifeboats, even though he knew that doing so would involve a considerable feat of seamanship in such appalling conditions. When the lifeboat did eventually manage to get alongside, in the best naval tradition Camille insisted that, as the captain, she had a right to remain on board until every member of her crew had been rescued. By the time it was her turn to scramble to safety up the rather unsteady rope ladder, Camille was so exhausted that she lost her grip and fell back into the sea.

Although unconscious when she was pulled from the water, she recovered quite quickly in the cruiser's sickbay and seemed no worse for her ordeal. Her new boat had been lost, but all the members of her crew were safe and Camille cheered up considerably on learning that she had been awarded the race, because her boat was the nearest to Toulon when it sank.

Camille was 72 when her adventurous life came to an end and she died peacefully at her home in France on 24 April 1942. She was not the first woman racing driver, as that distinction had gone to Madame Laumaille, who had taken part in the 1898 Marseilles-to-Nice race. She was, however, the first to prove that women racing drivers could compete successfully against the men, even under the most arduous conditions, and she did so against seemingly impossible odds.

Even so, Camille du Gast was remembered not only for the fearless way in which she raced cars and motorboats: she had a street in Paris named after her and she was also remembered by music lovers for the many brilliant performances she gave as a concert pianist. In the equestrian world she was noted for her fearless handling of the world-famous black Orloff horses she bred and rode so well, and throughout her hectic life she was always a great animal lover and an ardent supporter of many good causes.

She founded a dispensary for poor and sick women and also one for unwanted babies. For many years she was also president of the French Society for the Prevention of Cruelty to Animals and actively supported the refuge for stray and injured dogs that Gordon Bennett had created in Paris in 1903. He owned the *New York Herald* and was the originator of the famous motor race that bore his name. When Camille died, she left some of her great fortune to the refuge he founded at Gennevilliers.

2

The Racing Secretary

Dorothy Levitt was a long-legged beauty with unusually wide eyes, which gave her a rather mysterious Oriental look, and she had gone to the Napier Motor Company as a temporary secretary in 1902. While there she caught the eye of Selwyn Edge, the company's managing director, who was one of a small band of British racing enthusiasts who had been competing successfully in Europe, and had won the prestigious Gordon Bennett Paris-to-Vienna race that year in one of his company's cars.

While in Europe he had been impressed by the considerable amount of publicity Camille du Gast was creating for French cars and felt that an English woman driver, with similar beauty and talent, should be able to do the same for British cars, and his company's Napiers in particular. As soon as he returned home he began looking for a suitable candidate, and the woman he chose was Dorothy Levitt. She seemed to have most of the qualities he was looking for, because she was strikingly attractive, had a good personality and was keen to become a racing driver. The only problem was that she couldn't drive.

After making her his personal secretary, he arranged for Dorothy to be given lessons by Leslie Callingham, one of his company's salesmen, who later raced Bentleys at Brooklands; but young Callingham didn't relish the task of being her driving instructor, partly because the lessons had to take place on Sundays, which was his only day off. He also took exception to having to teach someone who, as he told friends, 'smelt of scent and wore large bracelets, unwieldy hats, silk stockings and innumerable petticoats'.

Dorothy's saving grace was that she learned quickly and had a natural driving ability, and Callingham was impressed by the confident way in which she handled a car. Selwyn Edge was relieved to learn that he seemed to have made the right choice, and set about turning his new secretary into a successful racing driver. His task was made easier because, in addition to Napier, he was involved with several other motor companies and they were able to provide different cars for her to drive.

Although motor racing wasn't nearly as popular in Britain as it was on the Continent, Dorothy's undoubted talent became evident early on in her racing career, when she won her class in the 1903 Southport Speed Trials, driving a works Gladiator, and the following year she was chosen to drive one of the two works De Dions entered in the Hereford 1,000-mile trial.

With sales dropping, the De Dion Company badly needed some good publicity and, as the only woman competitor taking part in the trial, Dorothy did her best to provide it. Although her remarkable flair for getting the maximum publicity out of every event annoyed the other competitors, it delighted Selwyn Edge and the De Dion directors. She had an eye-catching motoring outfit made specially for the Hereford trial, and the day before the start she posed for photographs alongside the De Dion, carrying her black Pomeranian dog, which snapped and growled at every driver who came near.

The following day, several photographs of Dorothy and her dog posing alongside the De Dion appeared in the morning papers and the other competitors hardly got a look in. They showed their disapproval of her successful attempt to hog all the limelight by arriving at the start with toy dogs strapped to the bonnets of their cars.

Having achieved the publicity she wanted, it was now important for her to show that she could drive as well as any of the men, and, with only one day to go, she looked like succeeding in doing so. Dorothy and her De Dion still had a clean sheet and she was in the running for a gold medal and top honours, when just before the finish her luck ran out and she was held up for an hour when her car developed a mechanical fault. The delay cost her the gold medal and on that occasion she had to be satisfied with silver.

As circuit races did not take place in Britain until the opening of Brooklands in 1907, Dorothy's early successes were restricted to speed events and long-distance trials, but, even so, in 1905 she caused a sensation by being chosen to drive one of the very fast 80hp Napier works cars in the very popular annual speed trials, which were held along the seafront at Brighton.

The Napier was a great brute of a machine with a distinguishing large square radiator and had originally been built for the famous Gordon Bennet race. It was painted British racing green and capable of reaching 100 m.p.h., so that keeping it on the road when going flat out presented a challenge for any driver. There were suggestions by some commentators that Dorothy wouldn't have the strength needed to control such a powerful machine and might even be killed if she went ahead and drove it in the trials. It was revealed later that a lot of the criticism had been stirred up by drivers who were envious that she had been given such a prestigious car to drive by the Napier Company. They felt it was only because she was a woman and the company was using her more for her publicity value than her driving ability.

If she was concerned about the criticism, Dorothy certainly didn't show it. The big green Napier looked immaculate as it was pushed to the start, and the crowd became silent as Dorothy's slim figure slid behind the large steering wheel and the car's powerful engine roared into life. She was dressed, as usual, in a smart dust coat buttoned up to the neck, with a matching hat and veil, and, despite the occasion, still managed to look a picture of elegance.

The cars raced in pairs according to their class, and the Napier was lined up against Moore-Brabazon's big Mors. As the starter's flag fell Dorothy was smartly away, accelerating through the gears with a dexterity that surprised her critics; and, with her foot hard down on the throttle, the big Napier roared across the finishing line at 72.52 m.p.h. She was even faster on her second run, reaching a speed of 78.7 m.p.h., which was quick enough for her to be placed third in one class and first in another and also win the coveted *Autocar* Challenge Trophy.

Even her sternest critics had to admit that she deserved her success and had handled the fast, high-powered Napier extremely well. The Tourist Trophy race that year was being run over the long course on the Isle of Man, and Dorothy was invited to drive a French Mors, which had been very successful racing on the Continent and was one of the favourites to win the event. Victory in a race like the Tourist Trophy would be undeniable proof that she was now a racing driver of the highest calibre; but, despite all her pleadings to be allowed to drive the Mors, Selwyn Edge objected strongly to the idea and wouldn't hear of it. His excuse was that it was not a suitable car for a race like the Tourist Trophy, but the real reason was that he didn't want to risk seeing a French company get the publicity a win by Dorothy would generate. His was a very selfish attitude, but Dorothy realised that she couldn't afford to go against the wishes of someone who had helped her get started and she also didn't want to do anything to annoy the Napier Company. In the end she decided to turn down the offer.

The Tourist Trophy race became one of the major events in the British motorsport calendar, but because it was a genuine road race it could not be held in mainland Britain for legal reasons and was always run offshore – in the early days on the Isle of Man and later in Northern Ireland.

Despite her annoyance at not being able to take part in the race, during 1906 Dorothy continued to drive the latest 40hp and 50hp Napier models successfully in hill climbs, and also took part in the much-publicised match with a steam car driven by Freddie Coleman. The steamer won, because it had the faster acceleration, but Freddie admitted later that in order to beat Dorothy and her Napier he had had to remove the stop pin from the steamer's pressure gauge.

Dorothy went to Germany in 1907 and was successful in the famous Herkomer Trial, named after the great German artist. It was the most important international trial to be held that year and involved several hill climbs and speed events, in addition to the usual long-distance aspect of the trial, when each car had to carry an official observer and cover a set distance within the time allowed. Dorothy and her Napier finished without any penalties, which did much to increase the prestige of women drivers in Germany. She also did her bit for British fashions by appearing at the prize-giving wearing a stunning outfit she had had designed specially for the occasion.

After being prevented from racing at Brooklands when the
track was opened that year, Dorothy went to France as a member
of the Napier team that took part in the famous Gaillon international hill climb. All three Napiers won their class and the
company's Grand Prix model won the event outright. It was to be
Dorothy's last important event. She disappeared from the
competition scene soon afterwards and concentrated on giving
demonstration drives for the Napier Company.

In 1909 Dorothy Levitt wrote a book, which she called *The
Woman and the Car*. It was described on the cover as a chatty
little handbook for all women who want to motor and contained
photographs of her that had been specially taken. When a new
edition of the book was published in 1970, Frances Howell
remarked in the foreword that there were now fewer women
competing than there had been in 1909, when the Ladies'
Automobile Club of Great Britain and Ireland had nearly four
hundred members, many of whom were competing in trials. The
club had its headquarters at Claridges Hotel and also a member's
garage.

Apart from popularising the sport among women, Dorothy was
the first woman to become a successful works team driver and the
first British woman to receive international recognition.

3

Women Drivers Fail to Convince the Authorities

When Hugh Locke King, a wealthy Surrey landowner, went to Brescia for the Coppa Florio meeting in September 1905, he arrived too late to see the race, but was shocked to learn that it had been dominated entirely by cars and drivers from France, Germany and Italy. There hadn't been a British car or driver taking part and the reason, according to the authorities, was that British cars and drivers were not considered fast enough. The drivers couldn't get the racing experience they needed in Britain, because there wasn't a suitable circuit and the government's strict speed restrictions made racing on British roads quite impossible.

As soon as he returned home, Locke King approached the Automobile Association, the Automobile Club and the Society of Motor Manufacturers and Traders, the country's three most powerful motoring organisations, to see what could be done to change the situation. All three organisations expressed concern that American manufacturers were also creating a world market for their cars, and, while British companies were keen to challenge the foreign-car supremacy in Europe, they couldn't do so effectively without a suitable race track where they could test and develop them.

Locke King then had meetings with leading motoring personalities and the media to tell them of his plans to build a motor-racing circuit on his Brooklands estate near Weybridge, which seemed an ideal venue. It was within easy reach of London and he had more than three hundred acres of woods and farmland available on which to build the track, all the facilities needed, and space for parking thousands of cars.

Work started in August 1906, about the time that the British concessionaires for Itala, Locke King's favourite make of car, began building an assembly plant on the estate. Colonel Henry Capel Lofft Holden, of the Royal Artillery, was put in charge of creating the world's first purpose-built motor-racing circuit, and plans were agreed for a huge concrete amphitheatre, which would have a circular three-mile racetrack 100 feet (30 metres) wide, with banked curves almost 30 feet (9 metres) high, enabling cars to race flat out at very high speeds in full view of the public.

The chosen site was a marshy stretch of ground alongside the London and South Western railway and more than two thousand labourers, most of them from Ireland, were brought in to fell trees, level the ground, build roads and bridges and erect more than eight miles of fencing. Scores of farm buildings had to be demolished, the River Wey was diverted in two places and seven miles of railway lines were laid to transport the 200,000 tons of gravel and cement needed for the roads. The choice of concrete was a bold decision, because it was not used for building public roads in Britain until some six years later.

Most of the men lived on the site in a shanty town of wooden shacks they had built themselves. Sanitation soon became a major problem and so did providing sufficient food and entertainment for such a large number of men living away from home for ten months. Costs escalated and the magnitude of the project nearly bankrupted Locke King and also came close to killing him. By the spring of 1907 many of his properties were already mortgaged up to the hilt and the money raised had already gone, not only on building the circuit, but also on several unsuccessful business ventures. He now didn't have the money needed to finish building the circuit, or the means of raising any more.

His poor health and desperate financial situation would have meant the end of the Brooklands project, had it not been for his wife Ethel, a woman of remarkable initiative and courage. She took over responsibility for raising the money and saving her husband from bankruptcy, as well as seeing that the work was completed on time. She was the daughter of Sir Thomas Gore-Browne, the former governor of Tasmania, and her family were not only very well connected but also extremely rich. Ethel persuaded them to help by pointing out that the failure to complete such an important project would reflect badly on both families, and, rather than risk any scandal, they provided sufficient money to finish the work. Despite all the problems, the circuit still took less than a year to build. It had cost more than £150,000 (the equivalent of nearly £10 million today) and was a brilliant engineering achievement.

The two banked ends of the circuit became known as the Byfleet Banking and the Members', or Home Banking. The impressive finishing straight, which was about 1,100 yards (1,005 metres) long, branched off from the shorter of the two level stretches of track to join the Members' Banking about halfway round the curve. It was built on a gradient to slow cars down before they rejoined the main course, but, although this worked quite well to begin with, as speeds increased the gradient became less effective and cars often ended up on the Outer Circuit until changes were made.

When the opening ceremony took place on 17 June 1907, it was Ethel, at the wheel of her Itala and with her husband Hugh sitting alongside, who led the forty-car motorcade of famous motoring personalities round the circuit. A few days later, on 28 and 29 June, Selwyn Edge demonstrated the value of the circuit as a proving ground for British car manufacturers by driving one of his company's 60hp Napier models a remarkable 1,581 miles 1,310 yards in 24 hours while averaging 65.905 m.p.h.

The first race meeting was held on 6 July, but even Ethel couldn't persuade the all male members of the newly formed Brooklands Automobile Racing Club (BARC) to allow Dorothy Levitt, or any woman driver, to take part. Apart from being worried about the effect women drivers might have on the macho image of motor racing they wanted to create, the BARC officials pointed out to Ethel that, as the Jockey Club didn't allow women jockeys, they saw no reason why they should allow women racing drivers. Selwyn Edge did what he could to persuade them to allow Dorothy Levitt to compete in a Napier, but the authorities remained adamant, even though she had the support of many of the media. The *Daily Express* gave wide coverage to the issue and provided a boost for women drivers by arranging for her to drive a London taxi round the circuit with several of her friends as passengers.

The winner of the first Brooklands event was H C Tryon in a 40hp Napier and the big race of the afternoon for the Montagu Cup and a purse of £1,400 was won by Jack Hutton, driving a modified 120hp Grand Prix Mercedes. With all the publicity created by Selwyn Edge's remarkable 24-hour record, Brooklands should have got off to a flying start, but that was not the case, and the first day's racing turned out to be a near fiasco.

Although more than 13,500 people passed through the turn-stiles and there were some 500 cars in the car park, the grandstand had been built to accommodate 30,000, and, with room for many thousands more in the enclosures, the place still looked rather empty. There were many complaints that the approach road was too narrow, about the high cost of parking, a shortage of food and a lack of information about what was happening; and, to make matters worse, the racing was dull. The track was so vast that the spectators had no idea what was going on, or who was in the lead, because they couldn't identify any of the drivers. The cars didn't have numbers and the only means of identification was the different-coloured smocks the drivers wore, which were similar to the racing silks worn by jockeys. Little wonder that it was impossible to distinguish one car from another when they were travelling round the circuit at high speed.

It wasn't until the fourth meeting there on 21 September that the situation started to improve, and, although the drivers continued to wear coloured smocks until 1914, every car now had to carry a large black metal disc with its number clearly painted on it in large white figures. Ebby Ebblewhite, who was the official handicapper and starter for more than thirty years, realised that, to get the close finishes the public wanted, every car would have to be handicapped according to engine size and performance. He was allowed to arrange for this to take place for the fourth race at the fourth meeting, and did so by marking the track out in yards and spacing the cars at intervals all round the circuit. That didn't work very well, either, because the starter couldn't see across the track with so many trees and buildings in the way, and, before the starting maroon went off, some of the drivers began creeping forward and gained an unfair advantage over those who stuck by the rules.

The obvious answer was a time handicap, which Ebby

Ebblewhite tried out for the June meeting in 1908. The introduction of handicap events and shorter races proved an instant success and attendances increased, partly because of these changes, but also because the admission charge was reduced to a shilling (5p). In addition, all the cars were more clearly numbered and the winner's speed was announced at the end of each race.

Unfortunately, the first fatal accident at the circuit occurred at the September meeting that year, when Vincent Hermon, driving Moore-Brabazon's Minerva, left the finishing straight too fast and overturned when it hit the Members' Banking.

During 1908 the finishing straight was used on several occasions by Alliott Verdon Roe for his flying experiments and in June that year he became the first British flier to leave the ground in a heavier-than-air flying machine. This provided a dramatic start to Brooklands' eighty-year involvement with aviation and successful record-breaking flights, after the Brooklands Automobile Racing Club, realising the considerable financial advantage to be gained by combing motor racing with the rapidly developing sport of private flying, had cleared part of the infield at the Byfleet end of the circuit and turned it into Britain's first aerodrome.

The first public demonstration of flying took place there in 1909, when the French ace Louis Paulhan made several flights with his Henry Farman biplane, including one with the intrepid Ethel Locke King as his passenger. Four years later another Frenchman, Celestin-Adolphe Pegoud, became the first pilot to loop the loop in Britain, when he visited Brooklands three weeks after he had performed the stunt for the first time at Juvisy, near Paris, on 1 September 1913.

4

Women Race at Brooklands for the First Time

By the summer of 1908 motor racing at Brooklands was beginning to draw large crowds and for the first time the authorities relented and allowed women drivers to race there. They were not allowed to compete against the men, but eight of them took part in a special Ladies' Bracelet Handicap during the July meeting. As a special concession they were allowed to wear coloured scarves to make them more easily distinguishable, instead of the coloured bibs worn by the men, but they still wore long skirts and as most of the cars didn't have any proper bodywork – because they had been stripped down to the bare chassis to save weight – this presented quite a problem. Several of the women solved the situation by tying their skirts down round their ankles with rope, to stop them from being blown up above their knees while they were racing, which might well have caused a scandal.

The winner was Muriel Thompson, driving her brother Oscar's

Austin 'Pobble', which went on to become a great favourite with the Brooklands crowd. She crossed the line just ahead of Ethel Locke King, at the wheel of the Itala 'Bambo' entered by Lord Montagu of Beaulieu. Third place went to little Christabel Ellis, who was so short that the top of the large steering wheel of G C G Moss's Arrol-Johnston 'Guarded Flame' came above her head, but she coped with the situation very well and added a feminine touch to the occasion by fixing a bouquet of sweet peas and cornflowers to the car's bonnet. Although the spectators seemed to enjoy the race and gave the women a great ovation as they crossed the finishing line, the officials of the Brooklands Automobile Racing club weren't impressed. They were still unable to accept the thought that women were taking part in a macho man's sport, and this and a match race at the August Bank Holiday meeting later that year between Muriel Thompson and Christabel Ellis, which Muriel again won, were the only races for women run by the BARC before World War One.

When war put a temporary end to racing in 1914, Muriel Thompson joined the Women's Transport Service and served on the Western Front between 1915 and 1918. She was in Flanders and was awarded the Military Medal, the Croix de Guerre and the Ordre de Leopold II for bravery under fire. Her well-known Cadillac also went to war, when it was converted into an ambulance and shipped to France to provide much-needed transport for the wounded. There is now a plaque in Ypres dedicated to Muriel and the other FANY's (First Aid Nursing Yeomanry members) who served there.

Although the Brooklands Automobile Racing Club had refused to allow women to race again at their meetings, several of the car clubs who held races there before the war did allow the wives and daughters of members to compete, even though allowing them to do so was still frowned on by the Brooklands officials. There was always a different atmosphere during those club meetings, which were informal family occasions and members frequently took their children along to the circuit. Ivy Cummings was just eleven when, in 1913, she was taken there by her father Sydney, who was a well-known London motor dealer and a keen amateur racing driver.

He parked their 15.9hp SCAR tourer in one of the paddock stalls and left his daughter on her own during one of the practice sessions, while he went across to the airfield to watch some flying. After he had gone Ivy started the engine and set off across the paddock towards the entrance to the circuit, slipping unseen past the officials, who didn't pay much attention to the car's driver. She had nearly completed a lap when a front tyre was punctured as she was entering the finishing straight and by the time she had reached the paddock the tyre was flat and it began to rain hard.

Ivy knew where the spare wheel was kept, but she injured her hand while trying to jack up the car. When her father arrived on the scene, he was so concerned about his daughter's injury and his wife's likely reaction when she learned that Ivy had been left alone, that he gave her little more than a mild ticking off. The incident did have one important effect on Ivy. Sydney Cummings began to encourage his daughter's interest in cars and took her to Brooklands on several occasions for driving lessons. He seemed quite proud of the fact that she was the youngest person to drive a car round the Brooklands circuit.

In 1916, when Ivy was fifteen, he gave her a small Peugeot car, which she used for giving rides to wounded soldiers and taking her mother and grandmother shopping, and Ivy was not much older when she joined her father's motor business as a driver, collecting and delivering different makes of car.

She drove a 1912 Vauxhall at the first meeting to be held at Brooklands after the war, and in 1922 won the Duke of York Long Distance Handicap race at the Royal Meeting there with a 1912 Coupe de L'Auto Sunbeam. Ivy went on to win many races, hill climbs and speed trials with a variety of very fast cars, including the legendary 5-litre chain-driven Bugatti, formerly owned and driven by Roland Garros, the distinguished French aviator. She named it 'Black Bess' after Dick Turpin's famous mare.

The Brooklands circuit was probably more famous before the war for the records that were broken there than for the racing, particularly when in 1913 Percy Lambert drove a streamlined, single-seater, 25hp Talbot to become the first driver to cover a hundred miles in one hour. After the war, however, Brooklands' influence on motor racing became world wide even in America. A party of Americans had visited the circuit soon after it was opened to see its design and construction and on returning home had built a less ambitious version at Indianapolis, which was opened in August 1909 and became the main racing circuit there after the war.

5

The Fastest Woman in France

Brooklands was also the inspiration for the Montlhery banked racing circuit near Paris, which became the home of French motor racing after it was opened in 1924. It was the scene of many successful record attempts, in particular by Gwenda Hawkes, a small, vivacious English girl, with a fierce determination she inherited from her Cornish father and Irish mother. She came from a family where danger was an accepted part of everyday life and courage was taken for granted, which no doubt accounted for her fearless driving and her remarkable record-breaking achievements on two, three and four wheels, some of which still stand today.

She was born in Preston, Lancashire, and her father was Major-General Sir Frederic Manley Glubb of the Royal Engineers, whose exploits during the Boer War and World War One made him the most decorated officer in the British army. Her brother, Sir John Bagot Glubb, was also a distinguished soldier. He was wounded three times while commanding the famous Arab Legion and received the MC, DSO, OBE and the CMG.

It was evident that Gwenda was not short of courage when she volunteered for the Scottish Women's Hospitals Organisation at the start of the war and drove ambulances during the thick of the fighting on the Russian and Romanian fronts. Her continuous bravery under fire was acknowledged by the Romanian government, who awarded her the Cross of St George and St Stanislaus, and she was also mentioned in dispatches.

She had learned to drive in a car belonging to a schoolfriend's parents when she was a pupil at Cheltenham Ladies' College, and was taught car maintenance by her brother, who was already a keen motorist and car owner. Her ability to survive while driving ambulances far from the nearest repair depot, along roads damaged by bomb craters and the heavy army lorries travelling to and from the front, frequently depended on her brother's training and her ability to carry out running repairs while under fire and keep her vehicle going until they could reach safety.

When the war ended she began to use that knowledge and experience to establish new speed and endurance records at Brooklands for motorcycles. The British motorcycle manufacturers became her first target and her remarkable record-breaking career started during the harsh winter of 1921, when in atrocious weather conditions she created a new 1,000-mile record with a rather aptly named Ner-a-Car motorcycle.

The motor-racing circuit at Brooklands would have been the ideal place for creating long-distance speed and endurance records, had it not been for the noise problems. After Selwyn Edge had created a new world record there with his Napier in 1907, the Weybridge residents obtained an injunction preventing the circuit from being used at night. It was at a time when there was still a considerable amount of hostility towards motorcars in

Britain, and, although the Brooklands authorities had the support of thirty other local Weybridge residents who confirmed that noise was not a problem, the magistrates decided otherwise. They even believed one woman who said that after the record attempt the strawberries in her garden tasted of petrol. Because of the injunction only double twelve-hour records could be attempted, with the vehicles locked away overnight between each of two twelve-hour record-breaking sessions.

In 1922 Gwenda made a successful attempt on the double twelve-hour motorcycle endurance record by averaging 44.65 m.p.h. with a 249cc Trump-JAP, and, while she was doing so, Selwyn Edge was also at Brooklands creating a similar record for cars with a very fast 5.7-litre Spyker. Gwenda's husband, Colonel Janson, was the managing director of the Spyker Company at the time, but their marriage didn't last and soon afterwards Colonel Neil Stewart, who was a well-known figure in motor-racing circles, became the second of her three husbands.

As soon as the Montlhery Autodrome near Paris was opened, Gwenda and her new husband left England and moved to France to be near to the Montlhery circuit, where the facilities for record breaking were much better than at Brooklands, mainly because there weren't any overnight noise restrictions.

The Montlhery circuit had, however, been modelled on Brooklands and the Stewarts were soon able to establish new 24-hour motorcycle records there. Not all their record-breaking attempts went smoothly and Gwenda had several narrow escapes while practising for them. On one occasion she was fortunate not to be seriously injured and to get away with just cuts and bruises, when the front tyre on her new Terrot-JAP motorcycle punctured during a high-speed run and the machine flew off the track out of control.

Gwenda's marriage to Neil also ran into trouble and it was

obvious to friends that she was having an affair with Douglas Hawkes, the talented motor engineer who had been brought in to help with her record-breaking attempts, and it came as no surprise when he became her third husband. He had prepared the single-seater Morgan that had been built specially for her planned attempt on the world speed record for three-wheelers, and in 1931 at Arpajon, a popular straight stretch of road near Montlhery, she drove the Morgan at an amazing 115 m.p.h., which remains an all-time three-wheeler record. She admitted afterwards that it was the most frightening drive of her life.

The same Morgan was used to create several other three-wheeler records, with Fred Cann, the son of the popular Brooklands gatekeeper who had moved to France to become the Hawkes's chief mechanic, fitting a different size of engine before each attempt.

Douglas Hawkes's controlling interest in the Derby Motor Company, situated just outside Paris, proved a great asset when Gwenda began racing cars during the early 1930s and particularly when he imported one of the very fast Miller Specials from America for her to drive. The 1.5-litre car had originally been built to race at the Indianapolis Speedway and was a similar model to the one in which Frank Lockhart had already reached a speed of 164 m.p.h. Douglas was impressed by the car's performance and knew that any records Gwenda achieved with it would also be good publicity for the Derby Company, whose models, like the Miller, all had front-wheel drive, which was unusual for cars in those days.

He was able to use the resources of the Derby factory to make several important modifications to the Miller, which included enlarging the engine to make it more suitable for record breaking, and from then on it became known as the Derby-Miller. Gwenda was not only a fearless and talented driver, but her mechanical knowledge was a great asset during the considerable amount of development work that had to be done on the car, which proved quite temperamental to begin with.

With Gwenda driving, the Derby-Miller broke many records at Montlhery, including the ten-mile and hundred-mile world speed records. She was about to make a fresh attempt on the outright lap record for the Montlhery circuit, when Douglas pointed to a button switch he and Fred Cann had fitted to the steering wheel and asked her to press it as the Derby-Miller was crossing the finishing line. They had wired the switch to cut the ignition while the Derby-Miller was travelling flat out, in the hope that doing so would enable them to get some additional information about the performance of the plugs.

When the Derby-Miller flashed across the finishing line Gwenda took her hand from the steering wheel to press the switch, but as she did so the car spun out of control and crashed at speed into one of the safety barriers. She was lucky to escape with only cuts, bruises and some broken ribs, but before the crash occurred she had created a sensational new lap record of 140 m.p.h., which no other driver ever came near to matching.

It was typical of Gwenda's careful attention to detail, probably the result of her military background and training, that even when there were not many people present during record attempts – apart from the usual official observers and timekeepers – she still insisted that her car be pushed to the start looking immaculate, half an hour before an attempt was due to begin. She also insisted that her two mechanics always wear spotless white overalls, which she supplied herself and paid for them to be laundered.

Despite all her record-breaking achievements, Gwenda never really made the grade as a racing driver. She drove a Derby sports car in the Le Mans 24-hour race in 1934 and 1935, but had to retire on each occasion with mechanical trouble. Her husband

Douglas also built a special Derby racing car, powered by a twin overhead camshaft 1.5-litre Maserati engine, for her to drive in European road races, but she had little success with that car, either.

Gwenda's main interest was always her record breaking. She claimed rather modestly that it didn't require any special driving skill and all she had to do was get in the car, break the record and then go home. The French government didn't think so, however, and recognised her achievements by holding a banquet in her honour and presenting her with a gold medal to mark the important contribution she had made to motorsport and the French motor industry.

After the fall of Paris in 1940 the Hawkeses returned to England and Douglas ran the Brooklands Engineering Company throughout the war. In prewar days it had produced engine components for the motor industry, but by the time Douglas arrived it was making munitions. As her own contribution to the war effort, Gwenda learned to become a skilled lathe operator and worked there on the factory floor until the end of the war.

The Hawkeses then left England for good, and, after spending a year cruising in the Aegean and the Mediterranean in their yacht *Eljois*, they made their home on the Greek island of Poros. Douglas died in 1974 from an advanced form of lung disease and, although Gwenda continued living in Greece, she made frequent visits to England, often driving alone across Europe in her little 2CV Citroën. When her remarkable life came to an end on 27 May 1990, she was only a few days short of her 96th birthday.

6

The Remarkable
Mrs Victor Bruce

Although Montlhery was newer and had the support of the French government, it never achieved the glamour and romance associated with Brooklands between the wars. Motor racing didn't restart at the Surrey track until 1920, because of the time it took to repair the damage caused by the solid-tyred lorries of the Royal Flying Corps squadrons stationed there during the war; but as soon as the circuit was reopened it became a major sporting attraction. Many young people now wanted to race cars, or fly aeroplanes, and thousands more went along to watch.

The first race after the war was won by Malcolm Campbell in his Lorraine-Dietrich at 84.5 m.p.h., but the atmosphere was different from the prewar days and the drivers, many of whom had survived four years of war, seemed to have a more relaxed approach to life. The cars they drove were either old Grand Prix models or aero-engine powered 'Specials' with hair-raising performances. Such as the big 350hp Sunbeam, which Louis

Coatalen had designed round a V12 Sunbeam Manitou power unit.

It first appeared at Brooklands in 1920, driven by Harry Hawker, the pioneer test pilot, and was the first car to lap the track at more than 120 m.p.h. The car was then raced by Kenelm Lee Guinness, a Sunbeam team driver, who in 1922 covered a flying kilometre along the Railway Straight at 137.15 m.p.h. – the last time that the land-speed record was achieved on a racing circuit. Malcolm Campbell then persuaded Louis Coatalen to sell him the 350hp Sunbeam and it became the first of his seven record-breaking Bluebirds. He took the land-speed record with it in 1924 and 1925.

The largest of the aero-engined racing cars was the massive 25-litre V12 Higham Special, built by Count Louis Zborowski to replace his aptly named Chitty-Chitty-Bang-Bang, but after he was killed in a race at Monza in 1924 it was bought by J G Parry Thomas, who fitted a new streamlined body and renamed it Babs, after his friend Archibald Frazer-Nash's younger daughter, Barbara Gabrielle. He was later killed in the car when it crashed on Pendine Sands in West Wales in 1927 during an attempt on the world land-speed record.

The fashionable restaurant and bar in the Brooklands clubhouse, now preserved as an ancient monument, enabled members and their guests to enjoy the lavish lifestyle for which the Roaring Twenties became famous, although the Blue Bird café the focal point for flying enthusiasts before the war, had disappeared. The café, situated in one of the hangars, had been owned by Eardley Billing, whose brother founded the Supermarine Company, which designed and built the seaplanes that won the Schneider Trophy race for Britain, and later produced the Spitfire fighter. It became a canteen when the Royal Flying Corps took over

Brooklands during the war but was burned down in 1917.

One aspect of Brooklands that hadn't changed since the war was the autocratic attitude of the officials towards women drivers. It was only when 61-year-old Ethel Locke King took over responsibility for running the motor-racing circuit and the airfield, after the death of her husband in 1926, that the situation changed and women were allowed to race there.

The first event for them was a two-lap women's handicap held in June 1927 and won by Miss M J Maconochie in a supercharged dark-blue Salmson at 87.22 m.p.h., from Miss H M Lister, in her cream, side-valve Aston Martin, and Mrs K Martin, in a black Riley Nine. After starting in scratch position, Mrs Jill Scott scorched round the circuit in the supercharged Grand Prix Sunbeam belonging to her husband, and, although she was unable to catch the race leaders, her lap of 112.68 m.p.h. confirmed that women were capable of driving fast cars as well as the men, and could no longer be ignored.

Another of the competitors that day was the Hon. Mrs Victor Bruce in her aluminium and cream AC, who personified the liberated women of the twenties and went on to hold seventeen world records. Whether racing cars, driving motor boats or flying aeroplanes, she showed a determination and fearless disregard for danger that made her a legendary figure within her lifetime.

The only daughter of Lawrence Petre, the squire of Coptfold Hall in Essex, she was born on 10 November 1895 and named Mildred May. Her American mother was a Shakespearean actress and her great grandmother had been by wagon train across the American plains with her husband during the 1849 California gold rush, fighting off raids by hostile Native Americans on the way.

In 1926 Mildred married Victor Austin Bruce, a grandson of the second Lord Aberdare. They took part in several expeditions and record breaking attempts together, starting soon after their marriage, with a 6,000-mile drive through Scandinavia in Mildred's AC saloon, which ended when they literally ran out of road in Lapland, 270 miles north of the Arctic Circle. Before returning they planted a Union Jack in the snow, but the journey was all the more remarkable because Mildred drove all the way.

After winning a Coupes des Dames in the Monte Carlo Rally and taking part in the first race for women drivers at Brooklands, Mildred went with Victor to Montlhery with their 1,991cc AC in December 1927 for an attempt on several speed and endurance records. Although Victor rolled the car over a snow-covered banking after only 147 hours, they still covered 15,000 miles and averaged 68 m.p.h. driving nonstop for ten days and nights. Both suffered badly from frostbite owing to the intense cold, but they still created seventeen new records.

Two years later Mildred returned to Montlhery with a 4.5 litre Bentley and drove single handed for 24 hours, covering 2,164 miles at an average speed of 89.4 m.p.h. She claimed later that she would have averaged 100 m.p.h., if she hadn't felt thirsty during a refuelling stop and taken a hurried drink from a Vichy water bottle that was on the pit counter, before realising that it was filled with petrol. Despite this, by the end of the 24 hours she had created a new world record for the longest nonstop solo drive and the newly formed British Racing Drivers' Club decided to elect her a life member.

When she was racing, Mildred refused to wear overalls or slacks, but was always dressed in a smart blouse and skirt, set off with a string of fine pearls.

'Don't call me a woman's libber!' she told one surprised interviewer. 'I don't approve of that sort of thing. I was a girl among five brothers and I have always tried to remain feminine.' That was another of her remarkable achievements.

After making the fastest Channel crossing from Dover to Calais in her powerful motorboat in August 1929, she then broke the record for the double journey, crossing from Dover to Calais and back in 79 minutes 24 seconds. Stepping ashore at Dover she told the waiting reporters, 'In future when I want to cross the Channel I shall use my speedboat instead of the Channel steamers, which are push-carts by comparison.'

The same year, Mildred created another new world record when she drove her motorboat single-handed nonstop for 24 hours, covering 674 nautical miles during that time.

Despite her record-breaking achievements on land and sea, there was concern in aviation circles when in 1930 she paid £550 for a twin-engined Bluebird aircraft she'd seen for sale in London's Burlington Gardens, then announced that, in spite of having done only forty hours solo, she planned to fly round the world alone.

Mildred looked a small and lonely figure when she set off from Heston for Tokyo on 25 September. The Bluebird had been fitted with extra fuel tanks and the pilot's seat raised to enable her to see out of the window. There were also two special items of equipment installed in the cockpit. The first was a wireless telegraphy set capable of transmitting a morse signal every fifteen minutes, in case she had to make a forced landing. The other was a dictaphone on which she planned to record her impressions.

The flight to Tokyo did not go according to plan. Mildred had to make several forced landings and on one occasion the wireless telegraphy set probably saved her life. She was delayed in Persia for several days when her twin-engined plane turned upside down while landing and had to have extensive repairs done before she could continued. She then became lost in bad weather on the flight to Istanbul and was missing for several days when she had to make a forced landing in mountainous territory.

When news of this reached London, a reporter suggested to her husband that some people thought he must be a 'funny sort of a chap to allow your wife to fly round the world on her own'. Victor only shrugged and said, 'If they do then they obviously don't know my wife. The very idea of my letting her do anything is humorous. When she makes up her mind to do something she just goes ahead and does it without taking notice of anyone. Her strongest characteristic is probably her determination and, the greater the opposition, the greater the determination. Some people would call it pig-headedness, but it is the quality which has been her greatest asset.'

Despite the various setbacks, Mildred reached Tokyo safely on 24 November, having made the first solo flight from England to Japan. Her return to London, during which she created the record for the longest solo flight, was relatively trouble-free by comparison. Her homecoming was hailed by the media as one of the most spectacular aviation events of the century and it was certainly impressive. Amy Johnson and Winifred Spooner were among a number of famous pilots who flew to Paris in twin-engined Bluebirds, similar to Mildred's own aircraft, ready to escort her across the Channel on the final leg of her journey to Croydon Airport. When she landed she was greeted by an enthusiastic crowd of well-wishers and it was obvious that her remarkable solo flight had caught the imagination of the public as well as the media. Mildred decided to take full advantage of all the worldwide publicity to form, shortly afterwards, her own aviation company called Air Dispatch, which she operated out of Croydon.

The new business venture didn't prevent her from making other record-breaking attempts and she again narrowly escaped death in 1936 during her record-breaking solo flight from India to

French Indo-China. She recorded the following poignant words on her dictaphone while she was lost in thick cloud over the Annamatique mountains and rapidly running short of fuel: 'If only I can reach some place and there is somewhere to land, I will be safe, but my petrol will not hold out much longer.'

Then, after a lengthy pause, she added, 'I shall not dictate any more now because I am too worried.'

Eventually she had no other option but to risk everything and put the nose of the aircraft down for a rapid descent through several thousand feet of cloud, but while doing so she still found time to record her feelings: 'If I happen to be killed this will be my end, so goodbye. I have done the best I can, but I am lost and if. I come through this now it will only be by the grace of God.'

She did survive and, after what she described as 'a really terrible experience', landed safely in a jungle clearing some twenty miles from the French Indo-China border, having created another solo flight record.

Still looking for new records to break, in 1932 Mildred bought an old Bristol Fighter and used it to carry out a series of experiments in air refuelling. Then, with a flying boat and the help of two co-pilots, she created a new world air-endurance record by staying airborne for 54 hours.

Her love of excitement knew no bounds, and the following year, having become bored with record breaking for a time, she paid £12 10 shillings (£12.50) for a single-seater Miles Satyr and a Fairey Fox bomber, both of which had been destined for scrap, and set off with them to join a flying circus. Then, after spending several months entertaining the crowds at air shows throughout Britain, she set her sights on another moneymaking project.

The civil aviation business was beginning to develop rapidly and new passenger aircraft were being built to deal with the demand. Mildred realised the opportunities and started a company delivering newspapers by air and running a regular passenger service between London and Paris. Daphne Vickers was employed by her as the country's first air hostess.

In 1937, when the War Office was looking for an experienced pilot who would be willing to fly through searchlight beams at night and provide the Territorial Army anti-aircraft gunners with some badly needed target practice, Mildred immediately volunteered and got the job. Then, with nothing to occupy her time during the day, she bought a horse and trained it to win the highly competitive Open Jumping Class at the Royal Windsor Horse Show.

When the war started she operated an air ferry service to France, but when that was no longer possible she moved to Cardiff and ran a factory repairing crashed RAF aircraft. By the time the war was over Mildred had achieved her final ambition, which was to earn a million pounds, so she decided the time had come to live a quieter life and moved to Bradford-on-Avon in Wiltshire, where she bought a large house, which had plenty of room for all her parrots and some of her favourite motorcars.

When Mildred was 81 and not having flown for 37 years she took a refresher flying course and celebrated her birthday by looping the loop over Bristol in a two-seater Chipmunk. Landing safely, she turned to her instructor and said, 'What a lark! That's knocked fifty years off my life.'

It hadn't quite. After driving home to Wiltshire, at what can best be described as a fast pace, in her favourite 1938 Rolls-Royce Phantom III Sedanca de Ville, Mildred spent the next thirteen years there enjoying life to the full, until she eventually died in 1989 at the remarkable age of 94.

7

More Records Fall to Women

The Cordery Sisters all raced cars, but it was Violet, rather than any of her sisters, who was the most successful and stole most of the limelight. She had been mad about cars from an early age and was taught to drive in the family Rolls-Royce by her brother-in-law, Captain Noel Macklin, who later produced the Eric-Campbell, Silver Hawk, Invicta and Railton cars. He married Lesley Cordery, and their son Lance also became a successful racing driver. Noel was later knighted for building the Fairmile fast motor launches used so successfully by the Light Coastal Forces during World War Two.

He had been badly wounded at the outbreak of World War One and, after being invalided out of the Royal Horse Artillery, secured a transfer to the Observer Corps. When he realised that he was entitled to have a driver, he chose Violet, partly so that he could continue with her tuition, but also to enable her to get more driving experience with several different makes of car. She put the experience to good use after the war when she won races at Brooklands with a 2.5-litre Invicta, which Noel had designed and built.

In 1926, although still only 25, Violet captained the team of six drivers who broke the world 10,000-mile record at the Monza circuit in Italy with a Newns-bodied 3-litre Invicta, averaging 56.47 m.p.h. The same car went on to capture the 15,000-mile record at 55.76 m.p.h., despite a five-day delay while repairs were made at the Isotta-Fraschini factory, after one of the drivers had fallen asleep and crashed the car. The Invicta continued to run a total of 25,000 kilometres (15,525 miles), taking more Class D records on the way. Violet became known as 'The Long-Distance Lady' when she took the same 3-litre Invicta on a Royal Automobile Club (RAC) observed run at Montlhery that summer. The car covered more than 5,000 miles at 70.7 m.p.h. and, in recognition of this and the other successful record-breaking attempts, the RAC awarded Violet and Invicta the coveted Dewar Trophy, for the highest motoring achievement of the year. It was the first time since its inception in 1906 that the award had been won by a woman.

In 1927 Violet set out on an RAC-observed world tour of 10,266 miles in a Cadogan-bodied 3-litre Invicta tourer. She drove across Europe, Africa, India, Australia, America and Canada in just five months at an average speed of 24.6 m.p.h., and the car went through six sets of tyres and inner tubes. Violet took with her a mechanic and a trained nurse, in addition to R W Sprague, the senior RAC official observer; but, apart from a broken half-shaft, the run was relatively trouble free and the Invicta arrived in New York on time. There was, however, one incident in Algiers when the Invicta was hit by a runaway tram, destroying most of the camping equipment that was being carried on the running board.

When in 1929 the Invicta Company wanted to prove the reliability of its car nearer to home, Violet and her youngest sister, Evelyn, drove a 4.5-litre tourer at Brooklands for 30,000 miles in about as many minutes at an average speed of 61.57 m.p.h. The record was supervised by the RAC, who again awarded Invicta their Dewar Trophy.

During 1930 Violet made another spectacular series of runs with the 4.5-litre Invicta, driving the car from London to Monte Carlo and back in third gear averaging 25.6 m.p.h.; then from London to John O'Groats and back in second gear averaging 19.8 m.p.h.; from London to Edinburgh and back in first gear at 12.5 m.p.h., and then fifty times round the RAC's Traffic Route without changing out of top gear while still averaging 11.9 m.p.h. Violet was dissuaded from taking the car to Brooklands and travelling 25 miles round the track in reverse as being too hard on the car, but a stunt like that might have stretched the tolerance of Brooklands Automobile Racing Club officials too far. The Invicta used in all the tests was the car that went on to win the Monte Carlo Rally in 1931 when driven by Donald Healey, who became the first British driver to win the event outright.

Violet's husband, John Hindmarsh, raced Talbots, Singers and Lagondas in long-distance races at Brooklands and in the RAC Tourist Trophy races, and he also won the 1935 Le Mans 24-hour race in a Lagonda, partnered by Lou Fontes. He was transferred from the Tank Regiment to the Royal Air Force and became a test pilot for the Hawker Company, whose main works was at Kingston-upon-Thames. They also assembled aircraft in their sheds at Brooklands, including the Hawker Hurricane fighter, which played such an important role during the Battle of Britain. John Hindmarsh was killed while flying a Hurricane from Brooklands in 1938, crashing not far from the circuit.

Although the Brooklands Automobile Racing Club refused to

allow men and women to race against each other during the 1920s, that didn't stop women from racing there at the many events organised by other clubs, and there were some outstanding husband-and-wife teams. Bill and Ruth Urquhart Dykes were probably the most successful and between 1924 and 1929 they broke several records. They had met while Bill was serving with the Royal Air Force in Ireland and piloted the aircraft sent to search for the Brooklands-built Vickers bomber that made the first west-to-east crossing of the Atlantic.

In 1924 Ruth began winning gold medals in long-distance trials with their first Alvis car, and two years later she made her first appearance at Brooklands, winning a gold medal during one of the most popular high-speed trials being held there. Then, in 1927, the Urquhart Dykeses bought WM 47, an Alvis 12/50, which had been returned to the works by a customer who didn't consider it performed properly. Ruth rapidly won three firsts, a second and a third place with it in short Brooklands races. When dry sump lubrication was fitted the maximum speed was increased to 95 m.p.h., and the following year Ruth gained a first and three seconds in Brooklands women's races.

The Alvis was then entered for several events in the Boulogne Speed Week, and, after being placed in a hill climb and two speed trials, Ruth entered it in the main event, which was a 300-mile road race for the Coupe Boillot. The race had attracted many of the world's top drivers, as well as some of the fastest cars, and, although she wasn't placed, Ruth became the first woman ever to finish the race. Members of the newly formed British Racing Drivers' Club were so impressed by her gritty performance that they invited her to become an associate member.

The Urquhart Dykes's 12/50 Alvis had already covered more than 100,000 miles when they made an attempt on the Brooklands twelve-hour record. Many people considered the attempt to be a rather ludicrous waste of time because the existing record of 80.06 m.p.h. had been achieved by a more powerful supercharged car and the 12/50 Alvis was unsupercharged and had a top speed of less than 100 m.p.h.

Ruth and her husband arrived at Brooklands at 7.15 a.m., made a few final adjustments to the engine and, after topping up the petrol, oil and water, Bill set off punctually at 8 a.m. to drive the first four-hour stint. Everything seemed to be going well until the engine cut out without warning after only three hours. Ruth rushed round the circuit in her Austin Seven to see what had happened, but by the time she arrived Bill had already diagnosed a faulty magneto. Collecting a replacement from the pits and fitting it cost them a valuable twenty minutes, and Ruth realised that she would have to make up the lost time during the next four hours, because her husband would be doing most of his next stint in the dark. After taking over, she had been driving for only about an hour when it began to rain heavily. The circuit became slippery, in addition to the normally bumpy surface, making it hard to keep the car under control. As the weather became worse there was a five-foot wall of spray coming up from the rear wheels, and the possibility that the Alvis might slide out of control and go over the top of the banking into the trees seemed even more likely.

As well as being able to see only straight ahead, Ruth found it impossible to read any pit signals, and, for the three hours that the storm lasted, the rain continued to lash her face and arms with a painful bullet-like force. Then, just before she was due to pull into the pits for the car to be refuelled and for her to hand over to Bill, the rain stopped. The possibility of making up any of the lost time during the storm seemed remote, but Ruth was pleasantly surprised to learn that she had been lapping at between 87 and 88 m.p.h. and they were now six minutes ahead of schedule.

Their troubles weren't over, however, and there was worse to come. After Bill had been driving for two hours it was becoming very dark, and Ruth and their helpers began putting out the eight road lamps, which was their only means of lighting the circuit, when the lights of the Alvis flickered a few times and went out. This meant that for the final two hours Bill had to average 85 m.p.h. in pitch-darkness with hardly any lighting. Doing so was a remarkable achievement and by the time the Alvis crossed the finish at 8 p.m. it had covered 976 miles at an average speed of 81.38 m.p.h. and set a new twelve-hour record.

The Alvis Company planned a full programme of events during the 1929 racing season for their revolutionary new front-wheel-drive model, which had an eight-cylinder, supercharged 1.5-litre engine. The factory worked flat out round the clock to get the new cars ready in time, and the only way they had of testing them was to wait until it was dark and then drive them round the streets of Coventry during the night, when there wasn't any other traffic around.

Ruth and Bill were invited to drive one of the new cars the company had entered for that year's Double Twelve Hour race at Brooklands. It was the first time that a top manufacturer had entrusted one of their works team cars to a woman for such an important race, and, although the Urquhart Dykeses finished unplaced and retired from racing soon afterwards, it was an indication of the high regard the Alvis Company had for Ruth's considerable ability.

8

A Lucky Gamble That Paid Off

During the period between the wars the women who raced cars came from a variety of backgrounds. Not all were wealthy and several made considerable personal sacrifices in order to have enough money to race, deciding that it was worth doing without fashionable new clothes, regular hairdos, expensive meals and visits to the theatre, in order to save money. A typical example was Victoria Worsley, who was being paid £2 a week by her father to act as his chauffeur, until a chance bet on a horserace enabled her to buy her first car and start her racing career.

Victoria's brother Willy, the popular captain of Yorkshire County Cricket Club, took her to York races and put five pounds for her on an outsider he had been given a tip for in that day's Ebor Handicap. The horse won at 20 – 1 and early the following morning she caught a train to London with her £100 winnings and drove home along the Great North Road that evening in a white sports Salmson. After doing a succession of odd jobs in the motor trade and swapping cars often, she made enough money to buy an MG, which she drove in the 1930 Double 12 Hour race at Brooklands, and an Ulster Austin, which she entered in the 1931 event.

Because of the rules still in force at Brooklands involving women drivers, on each occasion she had to have a man with her as co-driver, and the 1930 race became very much a family affair. Her brother Willy was the pit manager, a job he had never done before, and, apart from sticking out an occasional homemade signal for Victoria to go faster, come in to refuel or change over drivers, he spent most of the race sitting cross-legged on the pit counter taking movie shots. As well as the churns of petrol and cans of oil needed for refuelling, he made sure that the pit counter had a gramophone, plenty of the latest dance records, which he played throughout the race, and a good supply of bottled beer.

Victoria's co-driver was Derek Foster, the Warwickshire fast bowler, who was another MG owner and a friend of the family. Her choice of co-driver did, however, present one large problem. She was only five foot five tall, but Derek was six foot three, which meant that there had to be some very hurried adjustment to the seating every time they changed over. The chief pit mechanic was a naval lieutenant commander, who was Victoria's dancing partner and really more at home with ships' engines; but her travelling mechanic was more knowledgeable because he worked in the local garage and understood car maintenance. There was great excitement in the Worsley family when at the last minute the MG Company offered to lend Victoria one of their hotted-up works cars, along with a factory mechanic in case of any trouble.

As the race time approached, the drivers and their travelling mechanics lined up across the track opposite their cars for a Le Mans-type start, and Victoria's MG was one of the first away.

Early on, however, the race was marred by an accident to one of the very fast Talbots, which crashed, and debris littered the track as ambulances and firefighters rushed to the scene. It also began to rain, and Victoria's white linen overalls were soon soaked; but, despite the conditions, the MG gave them a trouble-free drive, and during the full 24 hours they covered just over 1,385 miles at an average speed of 57.72 m.p.h., finishing seventh in their class and twentieth overall.

Victoria competed in fourteen events at Brooklands between 1928 and 1932 with varying degrees of success, but the 1931 Double Twelve was probably the most memorable, not only because her Ulster Austin, with Lathan-Boote as her co-driver, finished seventh overall, ahead of the supercharged works cars, but also because an advertisement she had placed before the race in the *Autocar* magazine for a team manager also found her a husband. The advertisement was answered by Roland King-Farlow, a young accountant who had been helping Ebby Ebblewhite with timekeeping duties at the track. After marrying Victoria he became chief timekeeper at the Crystal Palace circuit when it opened in 1937.

Throughout the full 24 hours of the 1931 race, Victoria's Ulster Austin behaved perfectly and the engine never missed a beat, but, as they crossed the finishing line going flat out, the clutch disintegrated. She described it as 'a most gentlemanly little car to wait until then before breaking down'.

Jill Scott's introduction to motor racing was in complete contrast to Victoria's. Money was never a problem, because she was the heiress to a coalmining fortune and married to William Berkeley 'Bummer' Scott, a wealthy young racing enthusiast who spared no expense in ensuring that they both had cars capable of winning the top races. He even bought a large house at Byfleet so that they would be near to the Brooklands circuit, and they had their own shed at the track, where they kept their impressive stable of cars. The Scotts spent most days at Brooklands and between them must have covered more laps of the track than any of the other drivers who raced there.

Jill's husband had been to school at Fettes, considered to be the Eton of Scotland, and while there he had a series of fast motorcycles, which he kept hidden away in the local black-smith's shop and used them to go on illicit rides into the Scottish countryside with his schoolfriends. After going up to Cambridge in 1923, he became more interested in cars, and bought a smart Riley Redwing sports two-seater and a Benjamin, which he purchased from the proceeds of a successful spell of gambling. The Benjamin gave him his first experience of motor racing when in 1924 he entered it in the 750cc event at the opening meeting at the Monlhery circuit in France. He also used it for going to and from Calgary Castle, the family seat in the Isle of Mull.

Early visits to Brooklands between 1922 and 1924 with Phil Paddon, who had often sold cars to his mother, convinced Bummer that he wanted to be a racing driver, and soon after marrying Jill he purchased a 5-litre Indianapolis Sunbeam. Several Bugattis followed, including a 2-litre Grand Prix model, which he bought from Malcolm Campbell to drive himself, and a similar car, which he purchased for Jill to race. Like all their racing cars, the Bugattis were painted black with emerald-green wheels. They were wise purchases, because the Scotts had several successes at Brooklands and Montlhery with both of the cars and Jill succeeded in lapping the Surrey track at an impressive 117.17 m.p.h. in her Bugatti in 1928.

After J G Parry Thomas was killed at Pendine in 1927 (see Chapter 6), Bummer Scott bought two of his cars – the Leyland

Eight for Jill and the unsupercharged 1.5-litre Thomas 'Flat Iron' Special to drive himself. Both were different to control at speed and the Leyland Eight was not a suitable car for any woman to drive, even one as brave and talented as Jill. Because of this she let their friend John Cobb drive it in several races, and on one memorable occasion he lapped the outer circuit at Brooklands at 125.45 m.p.h. for three consecutive laps with her as his passenger.

Bummer fared no better with the Thomas Special, which was better known as the 'Flat Iron'. He was six foot tall and weighed more than seventeen stone, which made it almost impossible for him to sit in the car and cope with the controls. On the occasions when he did manage to squeeze his large frame into the cockpit he couldn't use full steering lock, because the drop arm under the dashboard rubbed his shin and the wheel took the skin off his legs. It was worse for John Cobb, who couldn't even squeeze his large frame into the car, and it wasn't possible to move the seat back because of the fuel tank, which was part of the tail. With Bummer having to admit defeat, Jill volunteered to try driving the 'Flat Iron', and she did manage to take some Brooklands class records with it, by sitting with her legs straight out so that she could just reach the pedals.

Jill and her husband were much more successful with the 2-litre Grand Prix Sunbeam they bought new from the factory in Wolverhampton. Together they notched up 53 wins with it at Brooklands and Jill became the first woman to be awarded the coveted Brooklands 120 m.p.h. badge when she put in a spectacular lap of 120.88 m.p.h. there in September 1928. The Scotts' daughter Sheila also lapped Brooklands at more than 100 m.p.h. in one of her parents' Sunbeams when she was only five months old, seated on her mother's lap while her father drove.

One of the Scotts' most memorable racing cars was the little 1927 black and green 1.5-litre Grand Prix Delage, which was also bought from Malcolm Campbell. It was memorable, not only because of the string of successes Bummer had with it at Brooklands and Montlhery, but also for a drive he made from London to Cambridge early one morning in 1929, in order to compete in the Inter-Varsity Speed Trials at Branches Park.

In those days, racing cars were frequently driven along public roads in order to get from one race meeting to another, but then there was far less traffic, no noise restrictions, no speed traps, or police cars lurking up side streets, and, by the time a village policeman had produced his notebook to take down the details of a speeding car, it was usually only a cloud of dust on the horizon.

On the evening before the Inter-Varsity event Bummer drove the Delage from its shed at Brooklands and garaged it overnight near his London flat. The following morning he set off early with a rather apprehensive Max Aitken, Lord Beaverbrook's son, sitting in the passenger seat, and as the Delage was fitted with trade plates, which were not allowed to be used in Hyde Park, they had to negotiate Knightsbridge, Park Lane and Marble Arch before they could get out of the West End traffic and take the road to Cambridge. Despite this they completed the journey in just 37 minutes. Bummer then recorded a sensational fastest time of the day in the speed trials by keeping his foot hard down on the throttle round the difficult final bend and crossing the finishing line in third gear at well over 100 m.p.h. He drove the Delage back to London later that evening.

Apart from being a successful racing driver, Jill was also a keen pilot, having gone solo in 1928 and purchased her own Avro Avian. Flying, however, was not one of Bummer's favourite activities, although he did sometimes fly as a passenger with his close friend Dudley Watt, who raced an old SE5a and other rather ancient aircraft, which he kept in a shed next to the one used by the Scotts at the airfield at Brooklands.

Watt was a flamboyant character and flying as his passenger took considerable courage, particularly as he enjoyed doing stunts, such as diving under the Byfleet Bridge at Brooklands. On one occasion he climbed out of the cockpit and on to the wing of his plane to prove to his terrified passenger that the aircraft could fly quite well by itself.

Watt and Bummer were due to lunch together at Brooklands one day, but when Watt arrived he explained that before they could do so he wanted to fly over his father's house and drop an important message, which he'd wrapped round a brick. The message was to explain that there had been a change of plan and he wouldn't now be returning home until later that afternoon. Unfortunately, however, the brick went through one of his father's greenhouses and the old man seized his 12-bore shotgun and peppered the aircraft with buckshot. The holes in the wing canvas were clearly visible when Watt landed and bore witness to the truth of the story and his father's accurate aim.

'Wouldn't it have been easier and less expensive to telephone?' Bummer asked as they sat down to lunch.

Unfortunately the Scotts' marriage ran into difficulties and during the summer of 1929 Jill met and fell in love with Ernest Thomas, a former RAF pilot who raced motorcycles and cars at Brooklands with considerable success and who was also a member of the Aero Club there. After divorcing Bummer, Jill married Ernest in October 1930 and their son Peter was born in May 1934.

Jill and her new husband departed from the Brooklands scene from mid-1930 until 1938, when they resumed racing there with a supercharged Alfa Romeo racing car and a Frazer-

Nash BMW 328 sports car. Jill's second marriage proved to be a very happy one and when she died in October 1974 Ernest was broken-hearted and died two months later. Their son Peter was only 63 when he died in October 1997, but despite his very adventurous life Bummer Scott was nearly eighty when he died in 1981.

9

Europe Leads the Way

Throughout the period between the wars, unlike in Britain, women racing drivers on the Continent were being actively encouraged to take part in the sport at every level. This was in no small way due to the legacy left by Camille du Gast (see Chapter 1), who had proved so clearly during the first capital-to-capital road races that women were certainly not wimps, or likely to damage the sport's image, and they had every right to compete on level terms with the men.

In France the petite and very talented Odette Siko became the first woman to take part in the gruelling 24-hour Le Mans race, although, while competing there in a Bugatti in 1931, she was unfortunate enough to be eliminated after 45 laps when, owing to a mistaken pit signal, her car was refuelled too early. Then, after finishing the race in an Alfa the following year, in 1933 she had a lucky escape while lying fifth in another Alfa, when just before dusk she misjudged one of the fast curves between Mulsanne and

Arnage. Her car skidded, went off the road, hit a tree, turned over and caught fire. Odette was fortunately thrown clear and it was typical of her quick thinking and courage that she seemed more concerned about trying to put out the flames and saving the car than about her own safety and injuries.

The cut and thrust of a race like Le Mans usually leaves little time for chivalry and the women certainly never asked for, or expected, any special treatment. The great French champion Louis Chiron loved motor racing and women and if both came together he couldn't resist using a little of his Gallic charm. Whenever he overtook a woman driver, or passed a group of women spectators, he always blew them a quick kiss. Had it been anyone else the woman drivers would probably have resented such action, but they knew he supported their presence there and so they usually smiled and waved back, as he disappeared into the distance.

Madame Mareuse had been Odette Siko's co-driver when they drove a Bugatti at Le Mans in 1930, but she is better remembered for her remarkable exploits in the tough and demanding Monte Carlo rally for several years running. On one occasion she had a narrow escape on the icy roads in Sweden, when the car she was driving was rammed by another competitor. Both vehicles caught fire but fortunately nobody was injured.

Susan Largeot, who was tall and dark and had the good looks of a film star, finished a very creditable twelfth on the first of the three occasions she drove at Le Mans, but little red-headed Anne Itier did even better. She was sometimes compared to Kay Petre, in that she was petite and full of charm and had a way with men. Both girls did become quite good friends when they were teamed up together during one international rally, although the only English Anne seemed to know was 'Kay, stop! Kay, stop!' She drove at Le Mans on five occasions, finishing eighth in an MG on the first occasion, then she was placed fifth for the cup in a Fiat, unplaced in an Adler, tenth in an MG and unplaced in a Simca. If things went wrong in a race Anne frequently didn't mince words and she wasn't afraid of using a few choice ones. Those were the occasions when her language was as fiery as her hair.

Another French girl who made her presence felt on the race track during the 1930s was Helle Nice, who took her motor racing very seriously. She was intelligent, attractive, very feminine and very French, and, although her appearance on the race track was always very workmanlike, she still couldn't resist shortening the sleeves of her overalls and sewing on a few little black bows. Even so, there was nothing amusing or particularly feminine about her handling of a racing car and many experts felt she did have the makings of a first-class Grand Prix driver.

Among the British women who did well at Brooklands, but who were also successful on the Continent, was the quiet but very talented Eileen Ellison, who could prove very difficult to beat at the wheel of a Bugatti, and also while driving a Lagonda and a Maserati. She didn't have much money, but managed to win the Duchess of York's race for women drivers at Brooklands in 1932 driving a Bugatti she had purchased very cheaply. Then she towed it to the Continent behind another Bugatti, which Eileen and her brother and a racing-driver friend had loaded with camping gear, cooking utensils and food, so that they could be as self-supporting as possible while driving to and from races and they wouldn't need to stay in hotels.

Living rough didn't seem to worry them as long as they were able to compete. Eileen's handling of her 1,500cc Bugatti during some of the long and difficult European hill climbs soon gained her the admiration of the overseas spectators and she became very popular with them. After a very hectic climb against stiff opposition on a very wet road, she was placed third in the famous Klausen hill climb and then fourth in her class in the very competitive Grossglockner hill climb, as well as having several successes in other hill climbs and speed trials. She was also popular on the race track with her Bugatti, holding fourth place in the Albi Grand Prix until two laps from the finish, when a fuel pipe broke, then going to South Africa for the Grand Prix there and, after being among the leaders for much of the race, eventually having to retire her Bugatti with fuel feed trouble.

After her motor-racing career came to an end, Eileen eventually settled in South Africa and bought a delightful villa near Cape Town. Apart from going on safari trips to the more remote parts of the country, Eileen spent a lot of her spare time swimming in the Indian Ocean and while doing so showed a total disregard for the possibility of being attacked by man-eating sharks. She always insisted that she was in no danger because she'd been told sharks didn't eat women!

The most remarkable and colourful of all the European women drivers was undoubtedly Elizabeth Junek, the sturdy little Czechoslovak who created a sensation in the 1920s driving her fierce-looking T35 Bugattis. They were all painted in the yellow and black livery of her newly founded nation and Elizabeth was always dressed in immaculate dark overalls with her familiar white cap.

The Targo Florio, which took place over 335 miles of dusty, mountain roads in Sicily, was always a particularly hazardous race, not only because of the sheer 14,000-foot drops and hairpin bends that the drivers had to contend with in the mountains, but also because much of the route was through bandit-infested territory. The 67-mile course had only one straight and that was the five-mile-long section near the coast at Campo Felice. The road surface was usually badly in need of repair, covered with loose stones and ankle deep in a dust that rose in blinding clouds during the race, obscuring the cars ahead.

Despite this, the Targo Florio was a race that held no terrors for the diminutive firebrand, who enjoyed taking on the best drivers in Europe. Driving one of the latest 2,300cc straight-eight Bugattis in the 1928, race she had a nose-to-tail battle for the lead with the French ace Albert Divo in a similar car. Their hair-raising duel lasted for 270 miles and ended only when Elizabeth Junek's car slid on some loose stones and bounced off a bank. Even so, she still finished a close-up fifth on the heels of Louis Chiron, the French champion.

Another woman competitor, that year was the German Countess Einsiedel with her 1,500cc Bugatti, who was going very well until her car also skidded on the loose surface going into one of the corners and hit a bank. The front of the Bugatti was badly damaged and seemed beyond repair, but after it had been straightened she continued in the race, although by then any chance she had of being placed had disappeared.

Countess Einsiedel, however, was not in the same class of driver as Madame Junek, who fell on hard times after her banker husband had been killed in his Bugatti while practising for a race in Germany, and she was seen some years later working as a mechanic in a tyre factory. It was a sad end for such a remarkably brave and talented woman.

10

The Flying Scot and the Girl from Dublin

Margaret Mabel Gladys Allan was a member of a well-known Scottish family where the women held strong views and were not afraid to express them. She had an aunt who was a suffragette and had gone to prison for her beliefs, and Margaret's mother laid down a set of rules based on her own beliefs, which the children had to follow. The Allans' considerable wealth came from the Allan Royal Mail Shipping Line, which became part of the Canadian Pacific Line in 1915, but Margaret's father was also a major shareholder in a project to build a teetotal paddle steamer, at a time when Clyde steamers were notorious for drunkenness.

She was born on 26 June 1909 and was sent to school at Bedales. Her holidays were mostly spent at home with the shaggy Highland ponies she learned to ride by winding her small fingers round their long manes and galloping round the fields bareback until she fell off. It was a hard way to learn, but it enabled her to develop an excellent sense of balance, so that, by the time she was big enough to start riding horses, she was already showing signs of becoming an accomplished horsewoman.

Her name might have been more closely associated with horses than with cars had it not been for her mother's insistence that everyone should make themselves useful, and it fell to Margaret to learn to drive the family car, so that she could chauffeur their guests to and from the station. Her mother had also instilled in all the family a belief that if a job was worth doing it was worth doing well, and within a short time Margaret mastered the intricacies of their 2-litre Lagonda and had become an excellent driver.

She'd become convinced that driving was something that women could do just as well as men and was annoyed to read that the women taking part in a trial organised by the newly formed Women's Automobile Sports Association had all shown a lack of skill throughout the event. After studying the tests, it seemed to Margaret that competition driving was an activity not so much for gifted experts as for drivers who were prepared to practise what they had to do and then make sure they didn't make mistakes. When the association organised another event, she persuaded her father to let her enter the family Lagonda and put her theory into practice. It worked, and Margaret won the trial and her first competition.

A visit to Brooklands followed and she drove the Lagonda in some of the club events there, but it wasn't fast enough for her to win with and it was not until she persuaded her father to buy her a larger and faster Lagonda that her racing career really got under way.

Her new car was fitted with a large supercharger, which developed a worrying fault during the 1932 Inter-Club Meeting and Margaret decided to take it to Robin Jackson, one of a number of highly skilled specialists whose tuning sheds were clustered round the paddock at Brooklands.

Left: The French beauty Camille du Gast and her mechanic taking part in the ill-fated Paris to Madrid race in 1903 with her very fast De Dietrich racer.

Below: In 1913, when she was only 11, Ivy Cummings became the youngest person to drive round the Brooklands circuit. This photograph was taken in 1923.

Bottom: Muriel Thompson and the Austin 'Popple' winning her private challenge match with Christabel Ellis, driving her Arrol-Johnston 'Blue Flame', which took place at Brooklands on 3 August 1908.

Left: Several of the women racing drivers were fine pilots, including Jill Scott, who learned to fly at Brooklands in 1927 and is seen here before taking off in her Avro 504.

Right: Violet Cordery created many new long distance records driving Invicta cars designed by her brother-in-law, Captain Noel Macklin, during the 1920s and 1930s and was awarded the coveted Dewar Trophy by the Royal Automobile Club.

Right: Gwenda Hawkes travelling at speed on the Brooklands banking in her Miller Special during her challenge match with Kay Petre to decide who was the fastest woman driver in Europe. The small propellor on the radiator worked an extra oil pump.

Below: The Hon. Mrs Victor Bruce at the wheel of the 4½ litre Red Label Bentley she raced at Brooklands in 1929, although she later became better known for her remarkable exploits in the air.

Left: Jill Scott was the heiress to a coal mining fortune and became the wife of W.B. 'Bummer' Scott, a wealthy young racing enthusiast who maintained a large stable of racing cars for them both to drive.

Below: One of the front wheels of 'Mother Gun' is off the ground as Margaret Allen comes off the Brooklands banking at more than 100mph in the very fast single-seater Bentley.

Left: The successful Scottish driver Margaret Allen, seen here in 1934 after winning the Ripley Long Handicap race at Brooklands at an average speed of 91.57 mph, driving her own 4½ litre Bentley.

Right: Margaret Allen and her future husband Christopher Jennings photographed together after announcing their engagement in September 1936.

Left: Fay Taylour finished her racing career in England and is seen here with a very youthful Stirling Moss before taking part in a 500cc race at the Castle Coombe circuit in October 1953.

Right: Fay Taylour was a succesful dirt track rider at the start of her career. During this race at the Munich Speedway, Germany, during 1930 she demonstrates the leg trailing style which all the speedway riders used at the time.

Left: After being taught to drive by the Hon. Mrs Joan Chetwynd, who had many successes at Brooklands, Dorothy Stanley-Turner drove a variety of MGs to win races there, including this Q type.

Right: Bill Wisdom always wore black overalls and a black helmet when she was racing, to ensure that they looked less dirty if she became covered in oil during a race.

Below: Kay Petre *(fourth from right)* lines up at the start of one of the many races she drove at Brooklands during her remarkable racing career.

To Bill with
pleasant memories of
Brooklands, Sincerely "Bill" Wisdom

Left: Mortimer 'Mort' Morris Goodall and Bill Wisdom, who were teamed up to drive one of the works Aston Martins at Le Mans in 1932, photographed before the start of the 24-hour race.

Above: Kay Petre hurries to her 750cc single seater works Austin before taking part in the 1937 Relay Race at Brooklands, which the Austin team won. During the race she was sprayed with hot oil from the reserve tank, but still kept going flat out to the finish.

Left: Bill Wisdom being congratulated by the Duke and Duchess of York in 1932, soon after she and Joan Richmond, driving a Riley, had won the first 1,000 mile race to be held at Brooklands.

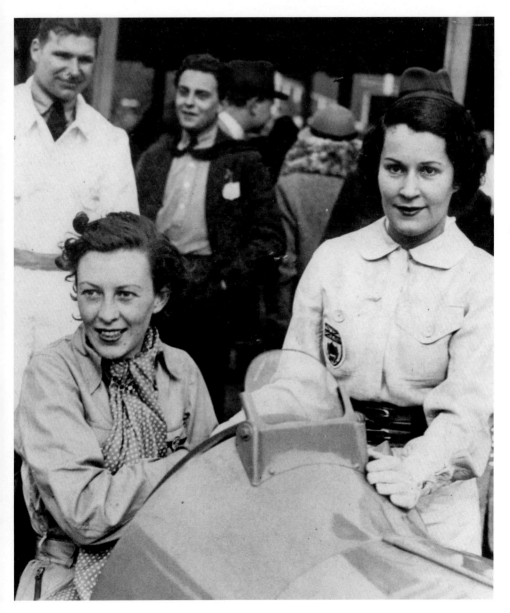

Above: Doreen Evans in the cockpit of her single-seater Q Type MG, photographed with Kay Petre before the start of a race at Brooklands during 1936.

Main picture: During practice for the BRDC 500-mile race in September 1937, Reg Parnell's MG number 7 suddenly stalled on the Byfleet Banking above Kay Petre's Austin number 3 and she was seriously injured in the crash that followed.

Left: The glamorous Kay Petre, wearing her favourite light blue racing overalls, is in deep discussion with Sir Malcolm Campbell before the start of a race at Brooklands.

Above: Although she was keen to return to racing after her near fatal accident, Kay Petre decided to retire after taking part here in only one race with her supercharged single-seater Riley, when she realised that much of the old dash and verve were no longer there.

Below: The popular Australian driver Joan Richmond at the wheel of the 3-litre Grand Prix Ballot she bought from Sir Malcolm Campbell to race in England.

Main picture: Competitors taking part in a ladies' race over the Brooklands Mountain Circuit in 1935. The line of trees at the edge of the circuit were always a hazard for drivers going too high up the banking.

Below left: A team of unblown MG Magnettes lapped at more than 100 mph to finish third in the 1934 Light Car Club relay race at Brooklands. Two of the drivers were Irene Schwedler *(third from left)* and Doreen Evans *(second from right)*.

Below right: A delighted Jill Thomas, after she had just created a new record for a fully equipped sports car by covering 101 miles in an hour from a standing start at Brooklands in her Frazer Nash-BMW.

Main picture: C.J.P. Dodson in Freddie Dixon's famous Riley leading the field during a 500-mile race at Brooklands ahead of car number 26, a Sunbeam driven by Charles Brackenbury. The photograph shows the the unevenness of the banking.

Above: Jill, and Ernest Thomas, who became her second husband, raced this Frazer Nash-BMW 328 sports car, seen here leading the field during a BARC race at Brooklands in 1938.

Centre: Doreen Evans lining up for the start of a race at Brooklands in her special bodied single-seater MG. She had a narrow escape when the car caught fire during the 1936 International Trophy race there, but escaped with only bad bruising and burns to her legs when she had to jump clear.

Bottom left: The Evans family's formidable team of racing cars lined up in the racing department of the Bellevue Garage at Wandsworth owned by Doreen's brother Denis. The famous 'Wilkie' Wilkinson prepared all the cars there.

Above: 'Bummer' Scott congratulates his wife after she had easily won a Ladies' Handicap Race at Brooklands driving his 2-litre Grand Prix Sunbeam. She later became the first woman to be awarded a Brooklands 120mph badge after lapping the circuit at 120.88mph in the same car.

Below: Jill Scott and her husband travelling flat out in their very potent 1089cc Riley during the popular Double Twelve race at the Surrey circuit in 1930.

By the time she had found Robin Jackson's shed he was already working on a Riley belonging to Christopher Jennings, a young racing driver who had seen the name Miss M Allan among the entries in the official programme and wondered whether she might be the girl he had met the previous year while staying with friends in Scotland. As soon as she came into the shed he realised that wasn't the case, because Margaret had dark hair and the girl he had met was a blonde. They turned out to be cousins, however, and Margaret and Christopher struck up a close friendship, which led to their marriage in 1937. When the war came, Christopher Jennings, joined the army, rose to the rank of colonel and had a distinguished war record; then, after demobilisation, he became the influential editor of *Motor* magazine during the rapid postwar development of the motorcar.

In addition to racing cars, Margaret competed successfully in several Monte Carlo rallies, driving a Rolls-Royce, a Triumph and an AC. She also won a coveted Coupe des Alpes in an Alpine rally, driving a hotted-up Wolseley Hornet Special with her brother acting as navigator. It was a nerve-racking experience, which she never persuaded him to repeat.

Margaret enjoyed taking part in international rallies, but motor racing remained her main interest until she married Christopher and decided to retire. The 4.5-litre Bentley she acquired in 1933 was much faster than her Lagonda and took some handling at speed on the bumpy surface of the Brooklands circuit. Even so, she quickly learned how to overcome the problem, and to everyone's surprise led the field to win that year's BARC Inter-Club race, putting in a flying lap of 97.65 m.p.h. It was the first of many successes she had with the car, also winning the Ripley Long Handicap in it that Easter at 91.57 m.p.h.

Although she was quite small, Margaret always preferred racing big, powerful cars and proved she had the ability to do so successfully. In 1936, soon after astounding the Brooklands officials by unofficially beating Earl Howe's 1,500cc Outer Circuit record of 127.05 m.p.h. in a borrowed Frazer-Nash, she was given Richard Marker's famous 6.5-litre single-seater Bentley 'Mother Gun' to race.

During that year's second March Short Handicap at the opening Brooklands meeting, she went through the field in the Bentley with comparative ease while lapping at 119.36 m.p.h., but the handicappers had badly underestimated the performance of many of the cars, and, despite her brilliant drive, she couldn't overtake the leaders. It was, however, an indication of her potential with the car and she went on to win that year's Whitsun Long Handicap at 115.25 m.p.h., becoming one of only four women to qualify for a Brooklands 120 m.p.h. badge by putting in a spectacularly fast lap during the race of 122.37 m.p.h.

Despite her successes with the Bentleys, the high spot of Margaret's distinguished racing career undoubtably came when she was chosen to be a member of the MG works team of three 847cc overhead-cam PA Midgets, which had been entered for the Le Mans 24-hour race by George Eyston. They were the first all-woman works team to take part in the race and their main objective was to perform well enough to qualify for the Rudge Whitworth Cup the following year.

They became known as 'the Dancing Daughters' and Margaret was teamed up with her close friend Colleen Eaton, an Australian who had a great sense of humour, but who was also a born optimist. The other members of the MG team were Joan Richmond, Barbara Skinner, 19-year-old Doreen Evans and Mrs Simpson.

Margaret and Colleen decided on a leisurely drive to Le Mans in the Australian driver's big Alfa, while the team cars were sent on ahead with the factory mechanics, whose job it was to get them all ready for the first practice session as soon as the other members of the team arrived. Although the practice sessions had gone well, on the morning of the race the members of the team left their hotel feeling rather apprehensive and arrived at the circuit just as the crowds were beginning to stream in. As there were some hours before the start, they decided to settle their nerves by having a picnic lunch and a bottle or two of French wine in a nearby hay field. The lunch and wine certainly had the desired effect, because they all fell fast asleep – and that was how some amused French officials found them.

By 4 p.m. and the start of the race the sky was heavy with the threat of rain and there were some ominous claps of thunder in the distance. The cars were as usual lined up 'in echelon' in front of the pits and Margaret and the other members of each team who were due to drive for the first session went across to their numbered circles on the opposite side of the circuit, waiting for the signal to run to their cars.

As the starter's flag fell, there was the usual wild rush across the track with everyone hoping to be the first away and praying that their car would start. One by one the engines burst into life and with a crackle of exhausts all the cars got away, with the exception of a lone Bugatti, whose red-faced driver was still trying to get it started as the others disappeared. The car's powerful engine coughed a few more times, then, to the obvious relief of everyone in the Bugatti pits, it also burst into life and the 1935 Le Mans 24-hour race was finally under way.

During the final hours of daylight and before darkness was to make the conditions more hazardous, the battle up front was as expected between the big Alfas, Bugattis and Lagondas. Then, strung out behind them along with the MGs, were the Rileys, Aston Martins, Singers, Delahayes, Talbots, some Frazer-Nashes, Amilcars, Fiats, Austins, a huge Duesenberg and a rather elderly Lorraine. The three MGs continued to appear each lap as regular as clockwork and Margaret was thoroughly enjoying herself until, as darkness felt, it was time for her to hand over to Colleen.

As she came into the pits, the storm broke and the rain came down in torrents. The corners on the circuit soon became very slippery, particularly the one at Arnage, and the clouds of spray coming from the cars in front made overtaking difficult and hazardous. An Aston-Martin crashed at the famous White House turn; a Riley slid off the road at Arnage; the leading Alfa went out of the race with a broken rear axle; and drivers and mechanics became soaked to their skin as the rain poured down nonstop for hour after hour.

Margaret and Colleen kept to schedule despite the weather, but when it was each driver's time to get some sleep they refused to use the official tent provided for the competitors, because it was already filled with men, most of whom were snoring away quite happily, and the organisers hadn't made any special sleeping arrangements for women. After she had handed over to Margaret and it was her time rest, Colleen headed for her Alfa, which was parked rather handily behind the pits. As she neared the car, she was surprised to hear snoring coming from it and found a member of the Bugatti team fast asleep in the back seat. The red-faced Italian was quickly sent on his way with some well-chosen words of Australian ringing in his ears, and Colleen took his place.

By the time the first grey streaks of dawn were appearing, a British Lagonda was in the lead and several of the larger cars had gone out with mechanical troubles, including the Lorraine and Gwenda Hawkes's rather temperamental Derby. Two of the Austins were missing, a Riley had caught fire in the pits and all the Singers were suffering with starter trouble. To the surprise of the crowd, who hadn't expected an all-woman team to last through the night, all three of the MGs were still running to schedule. The speed of the more powerful cars had fallen considerably, owing to the terrible weather, which enabled several of the smaller cars, including the three MG Midgets, to cover each lap at about the same speed.

As four o'clock and the end of the race approached, the Alfa driven by Lord Howe and the Hon. Brian Lewis seemed certain to be the overall winner, when, to the dismay of the British spectators, it broke a piston. But they had something to cheer about when the three MGs crossed the finishing line having run exactly to plan throughout the 24 hours. Margaret and Colleen had covered 1,576 miles to finish a very creditable 26th overall, but, even more important, all three cars had qualified for the following year's Rudge Cup.

As thirty of the starters had failed to finish, the British women had every reason to be proud of their achievement, but they never did get an opportunity to win the Rudge Cup, because the unfortunate troubles at MG put a stop to the company's racing programme and widespread strikes in France made it impossible to run the race in 1936.

Margaret had a son after her racing career came to an end and during the war was recruited to work at Bletchley Park, the secret government establishment responsible for breaking the German Enigma code. She was working in the Italian naval section there at a time when shipping intelligence was a vital means of countering the growing number of enemy attacks on allied convoys.

After the war, although no longer racing, she was elected an honorary member of the British Racing Drivers' Club and became motoring correspondent of *Vogue* magazine. When her husband Christopher died in 1982 she decided to devote all her energies to looking after her beautiful garden in Carmarthenshire, but she never lost her love of driving fast cars. She was well over eighty when the editor of *Autocar* invited her to test-drive three high-powered new models for a special feature the magazine was doing, but the day didn't go entirely as planned. Margaret set off for the Welsh hills in the first of the cars so fast that the magazine's photographer and the members of the editorial staff who were following in the other two cars lost her and all they could do was wait until she eventually returned. Even at that age the remarkable Flying Scot still loved speed and handled a fast car better than most drivers. She lived to be 89 and died on 21 September 1998.

Fay Taylour, or 'Flying Fay from Dublin', as she became known, was the only leading prewar woman driver to race cars after the war, when she competed in races in different parts of the world and was usually the only woman taking part. Attractive, well educated and with an aristocratic Irish background, she fortunately had the ability to 'talk the hind leg off a donkey', so that her frequent brushes with authority usually ended in a mild rebuke and smiles all round.

Regarded as being rather a daredevil, whether riding horses or motorcycles or racing motorcars, she combined a natural talent with a fearless approach to life. Fay began racing motorcycles while in her teens and after being a successful trials and grass-track rider, when speedway became a more spectacular sport and also more profitable, she turned her attention to that and became a major attraction at race tracks in England and Australia.

She began racing cars in the early 1930s, having been encouraged to do so by Brian Lewis, who later became Lord Essendon. After arriving unexpectedly at Brooklands for the BARC's autumn meeting, she surprised everyone by winning the ladies' handicap in a borrowed Talbot 105, lapping the Outer Circuit at an impressive 107.80 m.p.h. and holding off several of the established stars. In the same event at Brooklands the following year she finished second at 113.97 m.p.h. in Penn-Hughes's 2.6-litre Monza Alfa Romeo, which led to her first serious brush with the authorities there.

Elated by the experience of driving such an exciting car, she put in several more fast laps after the race was over and ignored all signals to stop, until one intrepid marshal who stood in the middle of the track frantically waving his flag eventually persuaded her to leave the circuit. Fay thought the whole affair was a huge joke, but the BARC officials were not amused and on that occasion no amount of Irish charm could save her. She was disqualified and fined, much to her disgust and called the officials 'a bunch of spoilsports'.

Her most popular success came when she won the Leinster Trophy Road Race before her home crowd in Ireland, driving a front-wheel-drive Adler 'Trumpf'. Again, she was the only woman competitor, as she had been when she drove a works Aston Martin in the Italian Mille Miglia. Spurred on by successes, she became a popular competitor at all the major meetings at Brooklands before the war, driving a variety of makes of car, from the small Salmsons to the big Bentleys, and won a women's race at Donington Park in a Frazer-Nash.

After women were allowed to race over the more hazardous Mountain Circuit at Brooklands, she borrowed a supercharged Alfa Romeo and broke the class lap records previously held by Malcolm Campbell and Raymond Mays. Her last race before the war was the 1938 South African Grand Prix, in which she drove Freddie Dixon's record-breaking Riley. He had been due to drive the car himself, but had had what he referred to as 'a little spot of bother with the police' and had lost his licence. Although Fay was unplaced, she got a great reception from the South African crowd for her spirited driving.

After the war she went to America to promote MG and Jaguar cars among the stars in Hollywood and while there took part in several sports-car races, which were new to the country. She also tried the popular American sport of midget-car racing on dirt tracks and enjoyed it so much that she toured the world competing in midget-car races with considerable success. The word 'midget' is rather a misnomer because many of the cars, like the Offenhauser, were very powerful machines capable of high speeds.

After returning to England, Fay raced a 500cc Cooper at Silverstone, Castle Coombe and Brands Hatch against brilliant young drivers such as Stirling Moss and Peter Collins, until, at the end of the 1950s, she finally gave up racing and retired to Dorset, where she died in August 1983 at the age of eighty.

11

The Race That Never Was

The greatest motor-racing hoax of all time took place at Brooklands and the novelist Barbara Cartland and a group of her friends very nearly pulled it off. As women drivers became more successful, some wildly exaggerated claims were made about them in the media. Some, like Victoria Worsley, complained that they were continually being accused of 'flirting with death' and 'dicing with their lives'. Even the least glamorous of them were described as 'ravishing', or they were 'dark-haired, blue-eyed beauties' and everything they said or did was blown up out of all proportion. Victoria told one interviewer, 'Actually, we are a modest, unassuming group of women, who just love driving fast cars and want to get on quietly with the job of doing so. Most of us are highly embarrassed about all the fuss being made about us.'

Their popularity, however, was looked upon with a certain amount of envy by some women, who longed to be like them and were envious of their celebrity status. That was why in 1931 a group of ten society women arranged to be filmed taking part in their own private race at Brooklands, but without actually putting themselves at any risk. Barbara Cartland planned the event following a remark a male guest had foolishly made at one of her house parties. She persuaded some of her friends to take part in the event to show off their driving skills and even suggested that the Society Ladies' Private Handicap might become a regular event at Brooklands.

Ten MGs had been borrowed for the occasion, which was filmed by British Movietone News. Princess Imeretinsky was to be announced as the winner with Lady de Clifford acting as her racing mechanic, and they were filmed crossing the finishing line a few feet ahead of the Hon. Mrs Joan Chetwynd, who it was claimed had been heavily handicapped because she was the only driver taking part who had previously raced at Brooklands. Third place went to Miss Paddy Naismith, who claimed the distinction of having driven the prime minister on several occasions.

Barbara Cartland and her friends got the publicity they were seeking and their hour or two of glory, until *Motor* magazine in its issue of 1 December 1931 revealed what had really happened. According to the *Motor* report, when each competitor arrived at the track she was issued with some white overalls and asked to pose in front of a row of MG Midgets borrowed specially for the occasion. The scene was then 'shot' several times by the newsreel cameramen and Barbara Cartland announced over the microphone that they were there to prove that women drivers were every bit as good as men. It was then decided that more still photographs should be taken of the competitors before they got into their MGs and drove off to the Railway Straight, where they were again filmed lining up on the starting grid. The handful of onlookers who happened to be there were rather puzzled that there didn't seem to be any effort to handicap the cars if it was meant to be a proper women's handicap, particularly as three of the MGs, including the one driven by the Hon. Mrs Joan Chetwynd, were supercharged and at least one other was brand-new and one of the latest models.

They were even more surprised when the starter's flag fell and all the cars, with the exception of one, which stalled because its handbrake was still on, tore down the finishing straight and began cutting each other up in a most alarming fashion for the benefit of the cameras. Since a large section of the Members' Banking was being repaired and there was barely enough room for one car to pass, even slowly, as soon as the cars reached that point they were forced to brake rather quickly. Princess Imeretinsky managed to get into a skid in doing so and spun her MG completely round, giving her what she reported later to be 'a delicious thrill'. Her passenger's verdict when asked about the spin was that it was 'too, too marvellous, my dear!'

The first part of the filming being over, it was suggested that the race needed a close finish and so everyone returned to the Railway Straight, where they were restarted, and, with the cameras whirring away, shot across the finishing line bonnet to bonnet. Princess Imeretinsky was then hoisted on to the back of her car while the other drivers gathered round.

A microphone was produced and she proclaimed to an imaginary crowd that she had 'derived infinite satisfaction from winning the contest'. Someone suggested that to add more realism to the film more shots of cars racing past each other should be included, and so everyone returned to the Byfleet Banking. The Hon. Mrs Joan Chetwynd, going as high up the banking as the car's top speed of 75 m.p.h. would allow with safety, was then filmed overtaking her somewhat slower rivals, and to round things off what were afterwards described as 'thrilling pit scenes' were acted out for the benefit of the cameras.

The *Motor*'s report resulted in a spate of letters condemning the event. Some blamed the Brooklands authorities for allowing it to take place, while others complained that it made women look foolish and was an insult to the genuine women racing drivers. One reader asked whether the 'so called society ladies' had expressed shame over their silly Brooklands escapade.

Mrs Chetwynd's letter was perhaps the most revealing. She wrote.

> I was told that a film was to be taken of women in sport and that a motor racing episode was wanted. I stipulated that no names should be mentioned and thought it would be just good fun. You can imagine my rage and despair when I realised what a farce the whole thing was going to be.
>
> I ought to have had sufficient presence of mind to refuse to take part in it when I got to the track, but it is difficult to make a fuss amongst strangers. I have never seen such a more shattering exhibition of driving in my life and count myself lucky to have come out of it unscathed. I think the people who loaned the cars were just as much led up the garden path as I was.

Joan Chetwynd, who died in October 1980, was a relative of Sir Henry 'Tim' Birkin and an enthusiastic competitor at Brooklands for many years. For a time she vied with the Hon. Mrs Victor Bruce as the most successful woman taking part in high-speed long-distance events. She set up a twelve-hour Class F record at Brooklands in 1929, when her 1.5-litre supercharged Meadows-engined Lea-Francis averaged 82.98 m.p.h., and in the 1932 Guys' Gala Meeting there she also won the Women's Automobile Sports Association Ladies' Race in another supercharged Lea-Francis.

She can also take credit for teaching Dorothy Stanley-Turner to drive and being instrumental in persuading her to take up motor racing. Dorothy's father was a wing commander in the RAF medical service who was friendly with many of the pioneer racing drivers, including Cecil Kimber, the managing director of the MG Car Company. It was because of this that throughout her remarkable racing career she drove mostly MGs.

Dorothy was a very attractive young woman with large blue eyes and with her looks had no difficulty in getting all the help and advice she wanted from the top men drivers when she began racing with a J-type MG Midget, built for the Le Mans 24-hour race, and also with quite a potent, slim, single-seater, Q-type, 750cc MG. Both cars were tuned by Thomson and Taylor, who built record-breaking cars for both Campbell and John Cobb.

She won the first running of the Easter Road Handicap at Brooklands during the 1937 Easter Bank Holiday meeting in her MG at 61.27 m.p.h. and showed no signs of being put off by the bad accident to Harry Clayton in the previous race, when his car went out of control and flew over the top of the Members' Banking. The first Easter Road Handicap was rather a milestone and an important race to win, because it was run over the impressive new artificial road circuit designed by Sir Malcolm Campbell.

There had been several important changes to the types of race held at Brooklands since the track was opened in June 1907 and its three-and-three-quarter-mile Outer Circuit, with its two steep bankings, was unique in the world and the only place where cars could be driven flat out for hours on end without any interruption.

The racing during those early years was always fast and exciting and the speeds attained on the circuit steadily increased. In 1908 the standing-start ten-lap record was already over 100 m.p.h. and by 1922 the flying-start lap record was more than 122 m.p.h., and it had reached 143 m.p.h. by 1935. Even the long-distance races were won at high average speeds and in 1936 the BRDC 500-mile race was won at 116.86 m.p.h., quite a remarkable achievement compared with the winner's average speed at the Indianapolis 500 in America that year, which was a relatively slow 109.07 m.p.h. Contemporary Continental Grand Prix races, run mainly on simulated road tracks, were even slower, with average winning speeds in the eighties.

In spite of the increased interest in road racing, the Outer Circuit races at Brooklands remained popular with spectators, but in 1930, when Percy Bradley took over from Colonel Lindsay Lloyd as clerk of the course, one of the first changes he made was the introduction of 'mountain racing'. The circuit used for these races was always down the finishing straight, right-handed round the Members' Banking, right again at the fork into a real hairpin bend and back along the finishing straight. Every testing mile and a quarter lap provided a cross between road and track racing and it was a tough course for the drivers and a stern test of the acceleration, breaking and road-holding capabilities of the cars.

As racing on that circuit continued to increase in popularity, in 1934 a new grandstand was built at the fork to give spectators a better view of the spectacular cornering during every race. Each of the five BARC events contained at least one Mountain Handicap race, and there were more in subsequent years. Because of the sharp corners, average speeds were lower than on the Outer Circuit, but even so the faster cars still touched 125 m.p.h. along the straight, and the Mountain Circuit lap record established in 1936 by Raymond Mays in his $1\frac{1}{2}$-litre supercharged ERA was a remarkably fast 84.31 m.p.h. The popular band leader Billy Cotton won the last race to be held on the Mountain Circuit, before the war brought an end to racing at Brooklands in 1939.

*

Until the opening of the Donington Park circuit in Derbyshire in 1933, Brooklands was for 26 years the only purpose-built motor-racing circuit in mainland Britain, but by 1937 Donington had become the venue for the important Royal Automobile Club Tourist Trophy sports-car race as well as an International Grand Prix, which brought to England the leading Continental teams of Auto-Union and Mercedes-Benz.

In view of the competition from Donington Park the BARC decided to construct a new circuit at Brooklands, which would provide the longest possible road-racing track without intruding on the aerodrome, or the famous sewage farm, often frequented by early aviators when their planes developed engine trouble, or the existing Outer Circuit and Mountain Circuit. The new course, designed by Sir Malcolm Campbell and named after him, was opened in 1937 by Dame Ethel Locke King and Selwyn Edge, who drove round in his Napier car. Following Dorothy Stanley-Turner's victory, the circuit became very popular and its design proved a credit to Sir Malcolm's knowledge and initiative. So much so that in 1938 it was used for the majority of car races and nearly half the motorcycle races held at Brooklands. The lap record was again set by Raymond Mays, who went round in his supercharged ERA at 77.79 m.p.h. By comparison, the winner's average speed at the first postwar British Grand Prix at Silverstone in 1948 was only 72.78 m.p.h.

After her unexpected win in the Easter Road Handicap, Dorothy Stanley-Turner's racing career took off. Apart from successes at Brooklands, she took part in long-distance races over the Donington Park road course and in 1937 also competed at Le Mans in a green PB MG, which she shared with Enid Riddell. They put up a remarkable performance by finishing second in the Biennial Cup category. Only bad health prevented Dorothy from competing there again in 1938, but as proof of her versatility she broke the women's record at the Shelsley Walsh Hill Climb, in Worcestershire, in a 2-litre Alfa she had borrowed from the factory and had very little experience of driving. Her final racing success was in 1939, when she drove her white Q-type single-seater MG to victory at the last race meeting to be held at Brooklands.

When war broke out Dorothy followed the family tradition of joining the Royal Air Force, although in her case it was the WAAF. In 1951 she married Air Commodore Geoffrey Tindal-Carill-Worsley and spent several years in the Far East during his overseas postings, although while she was away she never lost her interest in motor racing and kept in touch with her many friends in the sport. After her husband retired they lived in Somerset and on 8 July 1995 she died at her home there at the age of 78.

12

The Remarkable Evans Family

There was never any doubt that Doreen Evans would race motorcars. Her family's main topic of conversation was always motor racing. Her two brothers were successful racing drivers. All the family spent their free time at Brooklands and her parents felt that as soon as their children were old enough to drive they would be safer on a racing circuit in a well-prepared racing car than on the public roads. Racing was in her blood and Doreen's motor-racing career began in 1933, when at the age of seventeen she raced at Brooklands for the first time. It was a career, however, that lasted only three years and ended when she was twenty, but no other driver made such an impact on the racing scene in such a short time.

Her brother Kenneth always claimed that he couldn't remember a time in his life when he couldn't either steer or drive a car. His parents had been motoring enthusiasts from the early days of the motorcar and were regular visitors to Brooklands from the time the circuit was opened in 1907. They never missed an Easter Bank Holiday meeting and a particular highlight for the Evans children was being taken to have tea with J G Parry Thomas at his workshop in the Brooklands Village and being allowed to sit in his famous racing cars. Parry Thomas was very fond of young people and had endowed a cot at the Great Ormond Street Hospital for Children. He also named his world speed record car 'Babs' after his friend Archie Scott Brown's younger daughter.

On race days at Brooklands the Evans family picnicked on the Members' Hill and then watched the racing from the Members' Bridge. In between races Doreen and her brothers always rushed down to the paddock to see the cars and try to spot the famous drivers and get their autographs.

Denis, who was the eldest by two years, acquired a 2-litre Bugatti, which he drove in hill climbs, speed trials and club events, usually with his brother Kenneth as passenger. He also owned a two-seater Chrysler and a 2.3-litre Alfa Romeo, formerly raced by Earl Howe at Le Mans. The model was the forerunner of the famous 1,750cc blown Zagato version, which proved so popular in later years.

It became the custom in the family that the children taught one another to drive as soon as they were old enough to own their own cars. Denis taught Kenneth, then he taught Doreen as soon as she reached her seventeenth birthday. Until then she'd had to be content with being a passenger in her brother's cars when they were competing, but she now had one of her own and was able to start her own racing career with quite spectacular results for one so young.

When Kenneth left Brighton College and went up to Oxford towards the end of 1930 he bought a 1,500cc unsupercharged Alfa Romeo, which he entered in speed and regularity trials, and also drove in Brooklands club events with the wings and headlights removed. It was the first of a series of Alfas he owned and raced over the years, and he also purchased 'Buddy' Featherstonhaugh's 1,750cc supercharged Zagato model to use as a road car.

During the second year that he was at Oxford his brother persuaded him that they should take their motor racing more seriously and look for a more suitable car. They knew Hugh Hamilton, who worked for University Motors, and, as the new 750cc Montlhery MG Midget seemed to be the sort of car they were looking for, asked if he would demonstrate one to them. He agreed and drove the demonstration model so fast round the roads near the MG Company's Abingdon factory that the Evans brothers immediately decided that a Midget was the car for them and gave Hugh Hamilton a cheque.

Denis said afterwards, 'He nearly frightened us to death, the way he was driving that Midget, so for our good we decided to buy it and get the hell out of the place as quickly as we could!'

Since Denis had started the Bellevue Garage in southwest London in 1931, the emphasis there had always been on tuning fast cars, so it was the obvious place to take the Midget, particularly as the brilliant W E 'Wilkie' Wilkinson, later to be closely associated with Jaguars, had left L C Rawlence and Company, the main importers of Italian OM sports cars, to go and work at the garage and look after and tune the Evans family's racing cars.

London born Walter Ernest 'Wilkie' Wilkinson was a tuning genius, who went on to have a unique career in every aspect of motor racing from riding mechanic to Grand Prix driver. One of his customers at the Bellevue Garage at Wandsworth was Billy Cotton, the famous band leader who was a fanatically keen racing driver. During the war, when there wasn't any motor racing,

Wilkie tuned aeroplane engines, but he never lost his enthusiasm for motor racing and was 97 when he died in August 2001.

The first time Kenneth took the Montlhery Midget to Brooklands after it had been tuned by Wilkie, he was told to do a few laps of the Mountain Circuit under the watchful eye of Percy Bradley, the clerk of the course, to see whether he was capable of racing the Midget on the tricky circuit without being a danger to himself and the other competitors. It was a BARC rule that applied at the time to all novice drivers, but soon after Kenneth set off on his first lap it started to rain quite hard. He approached the celebrated fork on the course at what he judged to be a safe speed, but his car spun on the wet surface and continued to gyrate madly for some considerable distance, fortunately without leaving the road or crashing. As he drove back to the paddock, where the clerk of the course was waiting for him, Kenneth felt sure that his racing career would be over before it had really got started.

Percy Bradley gave young Kenneth a steely look, then smiled and said, 'Well, my boy! Let that be a lesson to you to drive more carefully in the wet.' Then he walked away and the incident was never mentioned again. Kenneth told his family that it was the action of a very kind and understanding man.

The Midget marked the start of a long and successful association the Evans family had with MGs and, as soon as Doreen had obtained her driving licence, she and her brothers all bought J2 MGs, to compete with as a team, mostly in trials and novice speed events. The new cars certainly looked the part with their low lines, cutaway doors, fold-flat windscreens, spring-spoked steering wheels, remote-control gear levers, centre-lock wire wheels and rear-mounted slab petrol tanks with quick-action filler caps.

Doreen and her brothers drove them successfully as a team in events and speed trials all over Britain, but when she decided to try circuit racing her father bought her a new MG Magna, powered by a version of the successful six-cylinder Wolseley Hornet engine, which went like a scalded cat with Doreen at the wheel. The Magna was tuned by Wilkie and gave Doreen the circuit-racing experience she needed. It also enabled her to catch the eye of Cecil Kimber of the MG Company, who from then on gave her and her brothers considerable support with their racing programme. Kimber was confident that the prestige gained by his cars in races one year would be recouped in sales during the next, which was the reason why, throughout the prewar years, so many MGs were raced by private owners at Brooklands and elsewhere.

It was a policy that certainly paid dividends, and, when the N-type MG Magnette was announced in 1934, Doreen and her brothers immediately ordered three of them in chasis form, with specially prepared, high-compression racing engines, ready to be fitted with the Evans family's own design of lightweight body. Doreen and her brothers then ran the cars as a team, taking on the official MG works team whenever possible, and they proved fast enough for them to do so with a considerable amount of success.

The cars were always carefully prepared by Wilkie Wilkinson, who was certainly proving a genius at tuning racing engines and seemed to be able to get more power from them than anyone else. He worked to the concept that racing cars were built to go fast and after he had tuned them it was up to the drivers to go out and win. As a result, none of the Evans family considered that driving well-prepared cars at speed on a circuit was doing anything dangerous. Their father Bertie always managed the pits with their mother acting as his very capable assistant.

All the careful preparation and attention to detail was undoubtedly the main reason why Dorothy and her brothers had so few serious accidents during their racing careers, but Dorothy did have a narrow escape when her single-seater MG caught fire during the 1936 International Trophy Race at Brooklands. She first noticed the blaze when she was going flat out down the Railway Straight and slowed down enough by the time she reached the end of the Members' Banking to jump clear. As a result of Doreen's quick thinking and cool nerve she fortunately escaped with nothing more than a bad bruising and some burns to her legs, but the MG careered on into the paddock safety barrier and was a complete write-off.

It was following her successes as a private entry that Doreen became a member of the official MG works teams, which were successful in the Light Car Club Relay Race at Brooklands and also at Le Mans. She also did extremely well with her own Q-type MG Midget and, after winning the Women's Mountain Handicap in it at Brooklands during the BARC's 1934 autumn meeting, had it rebuilt into a slim single-seater and won an Outer Circuit race at the Brooklands March meeting the following year, at a remarkably fast 101.77 m.p.h.

Her brother Denis gave up racing after his marriage and ran the family garage at Wandsworth, but Kenneth went on to become a successful Grand Prix driver. Doreen also retired from racing in 1936, when she married Alan Phillips. Her last race was to have been that year's Tourist Trophy Race, with Alan as her co-driver, but he crashed their Aston Martin on the first lap and she never had a chance to take part.

After their wedding Doreen and her husband settled in America and lived there happily for more than forty years, until she collapsed and died at their home in California in April 1982 at the age of 65.

13

Tommy and Bill Wisdom

Tommy Wisdom's marriage to the slim and attractive Elsie Gleed in 1930 marked the start of one of the most successful and lasting husband-and-wife partnerships in the history of motor racing, but it was Tommy's wife who proved the more talented. Although named Elsie, she was the only girl in a family of six boys and the name Bill was given to her by her brothers, who didn't feel that a girl's name was really suitable, when she spent so much time playing boys' games with them and their friends. Elsie also liked the name and insisted on being called Bill from then on.

Her first experience of speed came as a young girl, when she was taken for rides on the pillion seat of her brothers' motorcycles, but her parents gave her a motorcycle of her own when she was sixteen and it was a decision they soon came to regret. She rode it so fearlessly and with such enthusiasm that they became increasingly concerned about her safety, and, having decided that she would be much safer on four wheels than two, bought her a little friction-drive GWK when she was eighteen. The car got its name from the three motoring enthusiasts Grice, Wood and Keiller, who were responsible for its design and manufacture.

Bill tried using it in trials, but found it was nowhere near fast enough, and by the time she was 21 the little GWK had been replaced by a supercharged Lea-Francis, which had a top speed of 70 m.p.h. and was a much more exciting car for a young sporting enthusiast to drive.

Tommy Wisdom was a tall, good-looking young journalist and amateur racing driver, known as 'Tinker' to his friends, who at the age of 22 had been appointed motoring and aviation editor of a group of leading national newspapers and seemed set for a successful career in journalism. He met Bill under rather tragic circumstances when he and his brother were sailing with a friend one weekend off the southcoast of England. The friend was drowned when their sailing dinghy overturned, but Tommy and his brother were rescued and taken to Bill's house, which was nearby.

While Tommy was recovering on her sofa he saw Bill for the first time and in the weeks that followed fell madly in love with the dark-haired girl with the hazel-green eyes who had come to their rescue. The fact that she drove a supercharged Lea-Francis with considerable verve and skill and shared his love of motor racing also didn't pass unnoticed, and, when the Lea-Francis was replaced by a chain driven Frazer-Nash, one of the wilder sports cars of the day, Tommy was even more impressed.

Bill's Frazer-Nash went like a scalded cat when it held together, but it was also rather unreliable because the drive chains were inclined to break or become dislodged. Whenever that happened Tommy was usually on hand to carry out repairs and it came as no surprise to their friends when they announced their engagement and married.

They seemed the perfect couple, but there was trouble between them within the first few weeks of the wedding, when Bill learned that Tommy had entered her for the Ladies' March Handicap at Brooklands without asking her permission. She was furious and complained to friends that Tommy seemed more interested in motor racing than in her, but she was really less concerned about risking her neck in a motor race than she was about the possibility of making a fool of herself in public. That was really why she was so angry.

Tommy, however, dealt with the situation in the quiet, unflappable way that he did with every crisis that occurred throughout their marriage. The more he persuaded his wife that she had the ability not only to take part in the race, but also to do well, the more she became determined to win. She was even more determined when Tommy told her that he had borrowed a 1.5-litre Frazer-Nash for her to drive from his friend H J Aldington. She knew that the car was capable of lapping Brooklands at well over 90 m.p.h. and would be one of the fastest in the race.

Bill confessed later to friends that on the day of the race she did feel very nervous before the start, but all her apprehension and fear disappeared when the starter's flag fell and the thrill of driving such a fast car took over. The thought of what could happen if there was an accident did flit through her mind, but, as soon as she got used to the banking and realised how easily the Frazer-Nash handled the track at speed, all thoughts of danger left her. Far from stalling the engine when the starter's flag fell, which had been one of her main worries, she got away in fine style, leaving the other drivers strung out behind her to win by an easy three-quarters of a mile at 95.05 m.p.h.

Tommy was delighted at Bill's successful start to her racing career, but was not so pleased a few weeks later when they both drove the same car at the famous Shelsley Walsh Hill Climb in

Worcestershire, and Bill succeeded in scorching up the hill a full second faster.

It was the first of many occasions when Tommy had to admit that his wife was the quicker driver, given the right circumstances. Having tasted success, Bill now set her sights on more important events than women's handicap races and hill climbs, and, with the Junior Car Club's double twelve-hour race being one of the most important events on the Brooklands racing calendar, she was delighted to be given the opportunity of driving Aldington's Frazer-Nash in the 1931 race.

As usual it was a 24-hour event divided into two sections of twelve hours and run on two consecutive days, but that year the organisers decided that the cars should go the opposite way round the track, in the hope of eliminating the worst of the bumps the drivers had to contend with when coming off the banking.

Unfortunately, the change didn't work, and to make matters worse there was some very heavy rain during the first day, so the visibility was very poor. There were the usual spate of mechanical troubles, with Sir 'Tim' Birkin's supercharged Lagonda going out with engine trouble after setting the early pace and the Talbot team cars all having broken wing stays. An Invicta needed a new set of pistons, an Austin broke its crankshaft and one of the very fast Maseratis suffered a broken real axle.

The MGs seemed able to cope well with the conditions and were lapping the circuit faster than they had done in previous years, and Bill's Frazer-Nash ran beautifully for a while, until its main weakness showed up and it started throwing the final drive chains. She was eventually forced to retire, but being able to take part in such an important event so early in her racing career had given her some very valuable experience.

Tommy decided that Bill was now ready to have a crack at the women's lap record at Brooklands and took a calculated risk in buying the very fast, but also very unpredictable, 7.2-litre Leyland-Thomas single-seater that had been raced by Earl Howe. He was confident that Bill would be able to manage the car, even though several experienced drivers had already found it too much of a handful, and the Brooklands officials also considered it an unsuitable car for a woman.

They would allow Bill to drive the Leyland-Thomas in a race only if she could show that she was able to do so without being a danger to herself, or any of the other drivers. John Cobb, who took the world land-speed record in 1938, 1939 and 1947, was given the task of seeing whether Bill was capable of doing so; and, as he was known to believe that a woman's place was in the home and not on the race track, her chances of convincing him seemed slim.

She was determined to prove the Brookland's officials wrong, however, and not let their unreasonable prejudice against women drivers prevent her from racing the car. In order to prove her point she spent many hours going round the circuit at various speeds, learning how to cope with the disturbing habit such a powerful car had of wagging its tail alarmingly when going on and off the banking, unless the driver kept only the lightest touch on the wheel.

Despite his views on women racing drivers, John Cobb was impressed by the way in which Bill handled the Leyland-Thomas during the test run, driving it round the track at high speed and taking it high up on the banking before thundering down the straight flat out. She had done only a few laps when those drivers watching who were still hoping to buy the car saw their chances of doing so slipping away fast, and one humorist remarked that they slunk away to the clubhouse like disappointed vultures.

John Cobb was waiting for her when Bill returned to the paddock and, as she got out of the car, he laid his hand on her shoulder and said, 'Well done. As far as I am concerned you can drive that car at the next meeting.' They were just the words she wanted to hear, and John Cobb's decision was also welcomed by the other women drivers who had been watching rather anxiously. They felt it was another important milestone in their fight to rid themselves of the prejudice that was still being shown by some of the Brooklands officials.

The Brooklands Automobile Racing Club autumn meeting included a three-lap Ladies handicap to be run on the Outer Circuit. Bill was entered to drive the Leyland-Thomas, but having to start from scratch position in such a short race made it impossible for her to win. She did, however, put in a very spirited lap of 121.47 m.p.h., which not only set a new women's lap record, but also qualified her for one of the coveted Brooklands 120 m.p.h. badges. The new lap record was all the more impressive because of the heavy crosswind blowing at the time, which had the disturbing effect of pushing the cars high up the banking as they came from behind the Members' Hill, and making fast times more difficult.

Bill was fortunate in having Tommy's help before the start of each race and he always ensured that everything on her car was carefully checked down to the last detail. She also always looked immaculate, dressed in her black racing overalls and wearing a black crash helmet fitted with a sun peak. Asked by an interviewer why she always wore black she explained, 'Drivers get covered in oil and mud during a race and end up looking more like chimney sweeps. Because of this I find that I can look my best in black overalls and if there are a lot of cars on the track I also like to wear mask goggles, but I keep a visor handy for when there is driving rain.'

On another occasion when asked how it felt to be part of a successful husband-and-wife team, Bill remarked with a rather wry smile, 'It not only provides us both with plenty of thrills, it also gives us a never-ending topic of conversation.'

In 1932 she was partnered by Joan Richmond, the tough and amusing Australian driver, for the first 1,000-mile race to be held at Brooklands. It was the year when the Junior Car Club, later to become the British Automobile Racing Club, changed their annual Double 12 Hour race into one of 1,000 miles. It still had to be run over two days, owing to the noise restrictions, with the competitors' cars parked and guarded during the night. The race was also still a handicap, with cars of similar size going off together and the fastest and most powerful ones starting from scratch and going off last.

Joan Richmond was no stranger to long-distance events, having driven overland from Australia before taking part in that year's Monte Carlo Rally, and took her participation in the race very seriously. She spent several weeks at Brooklands with Bill practising with the Riley 9 they were to drive in the race, and, after discovering that it would lap quite comfortably at 86 m.p.h., decided that for the first part of the race they would attempt to lap at 85 m.p.h.

The driving instructions they received from the Riley team manager were quite simple. Watch for pit signals, press the lap scorer fitted to the facia board every lap, give a quick pump to the petrol pressure whenever necessary, give one pump of auxiliary oil every lap, and keep an eye on the oil pressure. Bill and Joan also decided to keep the engine to 300 revolutions per minute below the permitted maximum and go easy on the brakes until it was necessary for them to go flat out.

Bill drove for the first three and a half hours of the race and managed to average 85.28 m.p.h. as they had planned. Even so, when it was time for her to hand over to Joan Richmond, she was surprised to discover that they were in first place, although only a few seconds separated the leading cars. The mechanics put ten gallons of petrol into the Riley's tank and checked the oil before Joan set off and kept as near as possible to the average lap speed she and Bill had set themselves.

There were some anxious moments when the tie rod between the footbrake shaft and the gearbox snapped, making braking very erratic, and it was the cause of the two serious skids that Joan got into. Her experience of racing on the dirt tracks back home in Australia probably saved her from crashing, and she was fortunately able to deal with the skids and keep the Riley on the circuit. Although she was using the brakes as little as possible when cornering, the two skids had taken their toll on the tyres and she was forced to come into the pits early to change the two rear wheels, whose tyres were showing bad signs of wear.

The first half of the race ended after a few more laps and the cars were locked up for the night, with the Riley's engine sounding as crisp and healthy as it had done at the start. The good news was that another member of the Riley team was leading, followed by two Talbots, with Bill and Joan's car in fourth place, but there were still only seconds separating the leaders. That evening there was further excitement when it was realised that there was a reasonable chance of a Riley victory and that the two women were much better placed than they had dared to hope they might be at that stage of the race.

Tyres were their main problem and before they could set off in the morning the front wheels would have to be changed, the car refuelled and the broken tie rod replaced. Bill and Joan would almost certainly lose any chance of winning if all four wheels had to be changed again and it was essential that they should continue to use the brakes as carefully as possible and remember to ease the pedal right off every time the car leaped into the air after hitting the particularly treacherous bump situated on one of the corners.

Bill realised that the bump was the real cause of all the tyre trouble and told their team manager so, having spent some time the previous day down at the corner, watching the way in which the other drivers were trying to prevent their cars from being airborne for too long and the wheels from locking on impact with the ground when they landed.

Bill and Joan's Riley was due off at 10.37 a.m. on the Saturday and their three mechanics had the new tie rod and two front wheels ready to put on the car the moment the starter's flag fell. They had spent most of the night practising on another Riley to find the quickest method of replacing the tie rod and making sure that each man knew what he had to do. As a result, all the work that needed doing on the car was completed in a matter of minutes and Bill was still the first driver away in the 1,000cc class.

After three comparatively slow laps to allow everything to warm up properly, the Riley sounded better than ever and Bill's lap times were faster than those of the previous day. To her delight the signals from the pits also confirmed that everything was going well and that she had regained the lead, before it was time for her to come in to refuel and hand over to Joan soon after 2 p.m.

Even including all the pit stops their Riley was still averaging 84.23 m.p.h. and sounding as sweet as a nut, but tyre wear was still a worry. Their lead over the Talbot in second place was only three minutes, but Bill was pleased to see that, with only two hours to go before the finish, officials from the other teams were now beginning to look worried and anxiously clocking the Riley's lap time every time it went past the pits.

There was considerable relief in the Riley camp when Bill Freeman of Dunlop, who had been out on the circuit looking at the Riley's tyres through his field glasses, came back with the news that he felt they would last out the race. Despite that encouraging news, the remaining few laps still seemed agonisingly long, but the tyres did last and the little red Riley roared down the straight for the last time to receive the chequered flag and win Britain's first 1,000-mile race.

As the car passed the finish, the large crowd of spectators rose to their feet and roared their approval. Bill Wisdom and Joan Richmond had succeeded in beating some of the top drivers and works teams in Europe and had covered 1,046 miles at an average speed of 84.41 m.p.h., finishing a full three minutes ahead of the leading works Talbot in second place. It was a really polished performance and for women drivers to have won the first long-distance race to be held in Britain in such fashion was a tremendous achievement.

Joan Richmond stayed in England and had considerable success racing the 3-litre Grand Prix Ballot she bought from Sir Malcolm Campbell, but she returned to Australia after the war and was a guest at the fiftieth anniversary of the first Grand Prix to be held there. To her surprise, the Riley 9 was one of the famous cars on show, having been bought by the New Zealand driver Lindsay Wogan and shipped out to Australia for him to race.

Joan, who was proudly sporting her British Racing Drivers' Club badge, was asked if she would like to do a lap of honour in the car and jumped at the chance of driving the Riley once again. As she was climbing into the car, still looking slim and sprightly, although now in her sixties, Lindsay Wogan warned her about the large amount of oil in the cockpit.

'There always is,' she replied with a smile. 'I remember the car very well and my last drive in it.'

14

An Eventful Le Mans and a Disastrous Mille Miglia

Bill Wisdom's cool courage and outstanding performance while driving a number of different cars had impressed several of the top manufacturers, including the Aston Martin Company, which in 1932 was making a determined effort to win the Rudge Cup at Le Mans with a team of cars that were lower, had less wind resistance and were more powerful than any of their previous models. The company was leaving nothing to chance and as every car that year had to carry all the spares that may be required during the race, as well as the tools necessary to carry out minor repairs if there was a breakdown out on the circuit, it was important to have drivers who could diagnose and remedy problems quickly, particularly as the mechanics were allowed to work on the cars only when they were back in the pits.

Aston Martin consequently selected its six works drivers with great care and, despite protests about the inclusion of a woman in the team, chose Bill Wisdom to partner the experienced 'Mort'

Morris-Goodall. The other works drivers were Sammy Davis, who was driving with Bert Bertelli, Italian-born but a British subject and responsible for the company's design and racing policy, and Pat Driscoll, who was to be partnered by the good-natured Penn Hughes.

Preparations for the race went according to plan, with Bill insisting on being treated exactly the same as the other members of the Aston Martin team. She knew that her selection was partly an experiment, to see whether a woman could fit into a top racing team without causing any problems, or creating the wrong sort of publicity. There was never any doubt that she would be able to handle the new Aston Martin, particularly in view of the way she had been racing the very fast, but rather unpredictable, Leyland-Thomas so successfully.

A few days before the race, all the drivers and the team manager went over to France, together with the three team cars and their truck, two standard Aston Martins for use as runabouts, a chart keeper, mechanics, signallers, spotters and all the usual paraphernalia associated with a major international racing team. Everyone enjoyed the picnic lunch, which was eaten by the roadside French style, and there was a general feeling of excitement when they reached Le Mans early that evening and booked into their hotel. The nearby garage that had been reserved for the cars seemed fine, until someone noticed that one of the lockups had '13' on the door, but the problem was solved by having the number hastily painted out before the remaining team car was locked away inside.

Everything seemed to be going well the following day, except that an overenthusiastic Mort Morris-Goodall was as usual rather accident-prone. First of all, he was hit in the eye by a rather angry wasp while the drivers were out learning the circuit, and shortly afterwards he was lucky to escape injury when he fell out of the team truck, accompanied by several large fuel cans, while it was parked in the hotel yard. There was a general feeling of relief, particularly from Bill, when Mort's wife Vanne arrived and made sure that her rather boisterous husband kept out of any further trouble.

Mort's considerable racing experience gave Bill the additional confidence she needed for her first drive for the Aston Martin team, particularly as they were in LM7, his favourite car and one which he knew well.

After being an apprentice with the Sunbeam Motor Company, Mort had begun his racing career at Brooklands in 1929 and went on to compete in every Le Mans 24 hour race from 1931 until the war. Even then he couldn't keep away from the place and while in France with the British Expeditionary Force in 1940 he lapped the circuit in an army truck. He raced again at Le Mans after the war, competing more times in the race than any other British driver and was 95 when he died on 14 May 2001.

The 1932 race started with the usual dash to the cars at four o'clock on the Saturday afternoon, and within a few hours it was obvious that the Astons were running well and had the necessary speed to win. While Mort Morris-Goodall was doing the first stint, Bill was kept occupied looking after a small bird, which must have made a nest in the pits some time before the race was due to take place. The team named it 'Fifi' and it seemed to be oblivious of all the bustle and excitement going on, but went on feeding its young family as though nothing unusual were taking place. All the lap charts, fuel cans and other paraphernalia were cleared away from the vicinity of the nest and Bill was detailed to look after Fifi's general wellbeing and make sure that she had a plentiful supply of food.

The bird's antics had a soothing effect on everyone's nerves and, although Bill had been fretting before the race as to whether she would be able to keep up the scheduled speed, or might do something silly, all her worries disappeared as soon as she took over from Mort and got behind the wheel of the Aston. The orders were that when drivers came into the pits to hand over they should help the mechanics to refill the cars with oil, water and fuel and give their co-drivers advice on the state of the track and anything that may need watching on their cars. The problem was that each time the refuelling took place the officials had to reseal the petrol filler caps before the car could restart. This was sometimes a slower process than the drivers and pit staff felt necessary and led to some angry words.

The information Bill received from Mort about the car and the track, when it was her turn to drive, proved very useful and as dusk approached she was relaxed, enjoying herself and driving like a veteran. The car being driven by Bert Bertelli and Sammy Davis had been built to be lighter and was consequently faster, which was part of the team's tactics for the race. It could lap more quickly than the other two team cars, and twice when Sammy Davis was driving he followed Bill into a corner and was impressed by how fast she took it and then how quickly she pulled over to let his faster car pass, which was a sign of good driving manners and the proper use of the car's mirrors. Bill even managed to give Sammy a quick wave as he disappeared into the distance.

When she came into the pits to hand over to Mort, Sammy was pleased to see how well Bill coped with the refuelling process, knowing full well that the mechanics were watching to see how she performed. It was dark when Bill went out for her second stint at the wheel and, although the thought of having to drive the Aston flat out during the night for the first time could have been rather nerve-racking, she dealt with the situation very well. Everything was going according to plan and Bill was driving the

Aston down the long straight, when suddenly there was a loud bang and the engine seemed to disintegrate. It was discovered later that a faulty cap for one of the crank bearings had caused the problem, which was something that had never happened before and couldn't be blamed on the driver.

There was nothing Bill could do but pull over on to the verge, leave the car and set off rather despondently in the direction of the pits. When Sammy Davis saw the Aston on the grass he was worried about the driver, but, as there was no sign of the ambulance, he assumed that Bill was all right and that her car must have been put out of the race by mechanical trouble.

On her way back to the pits Bill was met by an official, who wanted to know what had happened. Unable to remember much of her limited French in the heat of the moment, she waved her arms in the air and said, 'Voiture bang! Voiture bang!', which suggested to the worried official that she had crashed, and he insisted that Bill should be examined immediately by a course doctor. Despite her obvious resistance to the suggestion, he led her to a first-aid tent. When she realised that a full medical examination was about to take place, she resisted even harder. The suspicions Bill had about French medical examinations were based on the rather lurid stories she had heard from the other drivers, and she had no intention of letting the same thing happen to her. Eventually, the officials and the doctor came to the conclusion that they were dealing with an eccentric English woman who couldn't have been hurt too badly, or she wouldn't be making such a fuss; and with a sense of relief they let her go. Bill returned to the Aston pits, pleased to have escaped the clutches of the French doctors, and glad at last to be able to tell Mort and her team manager what had happened to the car.

Although the engine failure in the Le Mans race was a big disappointment, Bill had better luck in the Junior Car Club's

International Trophy Race at Brooklands, which took place soon afterwards. She was the only woman driver and had an excellent chance of doing well, particularly as she had been given one of the new MG Magnettes to drive. The race was different that year because of the novel method of handicapping, which was intended to even out the chances of winning for the various makes and sizes of car taking part. Instead of handicapping by time, which was the usual way, the cars in each class were given a different route to follow according to their engine size. It was a method of handicapping that could have been done only at Brooklands, where the width of the track near the Vickers shed allowed three groups of corners to be laid out and marked by barriers. Each class was then allotted its own corner.

Everyone started together, but the trouble began on the first lap, when one MG went out with engine trouble, another skidded into the bank on one of the turns and George Eyston's very fast Midget lost a front wheel. It looked as though Horton's MG would win, but then it also developed engine trouble. Malcolm Campbell's Sunbeam went to the front, but his lead was short-lived, and, when Ross Richard's big Bugatti seemed like being the winner, its rear axle broke. Whitney Straight took the lead with his Maserati and managed to stay there until driving with rather too much verve put him out of the race.

It seemed to Bill that many of the cars that were making the expensive noises were the same make and size as hers, and at one stage the air seemed filled with bits of flying metal, and there were more pieces of car lying on the track. There had never been so much trouble during a race at Brooklands, or so many broken cranks, piston rods going through crank cases and pistons collapsing. There were even instances of shock absorbers falling off. Only eight of the starters survived, including Bill's Magnette, which under the circumstances finished a very creditable third at 81.24 m.p.h.

In addition to being a racing driver, Bill was having to run a home, look after her husband and bring up their young daughter Anne, who could often be seen at Brooklands playing in the paddock with her toy car, while her mother was out on the circuit practising. Tommy and Bill were immensely proud when, after the war, Anne, or 'Wiz' as she was known to her team-mates, became a top international rally driver.

In 1934 competition was fierce among the women drivers to create a new Outer Circuit lap record at Brooklands, and Bill persuaded the fiery and sometimes temperamental Freddie Dixon to let her borrow his own specially tuned Riley for her attempt. He agreed on condition that she take the car out for three laps in the morning and three in the afternoon – and that would be all.

When Bill went out in the morning, she was conscious that Freddie was watching her very carefully, but she was relieved to find that the Riley was easier to handle at speed than she had thought might be the case. The only problem was that every time it went over a bump – and there were many – she was thrown up in the air and had difficulty staying in the cockpit.

On the second lap there was a loud bang and something hit her right elbow very hard. For several hectic seconds she struggled to keep the car under control and, when she pulled into the pits, it was obvious that a rear tread had come loose and was acting as a high-speed flail, striking her arm with considerable force every time she was unable to get it out of the way in time. Freddie Dixon looked as though he were about to explode, despite the tears of pain in Bill's eyes, until Dunlop Mac, the tyre company's popular racing manager, who had seen what had happened, saved the situation by rushing up and congratulating Bill on her brilliant handling of the car at speed under such frightening circumstances.

After that Freddie cooled down and promised to let Bill have another go in the afternoon. New tyres were fitted and she was given a makeshift harness to hold her down in the cockpit when the car became airborne over the bumps. To her relief and Freddie's delight, Bill then went out and put in a lap of 126.73 m.p.h. to create a new women's lap record.

The high spot of the 1935 season at Brooklands was the International Trophy run on Jubilee Day, and Tommy and Bill shared the wheel of a Riley for the race. Although driving together as a husband-and-wife team in an event of that importance might provide grounds for divorce with some couples and lead to the break-up of a marriage, the Wisdoms had such confidence in each other's driving ability, and both had such a great sense of humour, that there was never any risk that such a thing would happen when they teamed up together.

The race ran true to form. A new-model MG was beset with teething troubles and even before the start there were heavy casualties among the cars during the practice sessions. As usual, the Brooklands bumps proved the most unpredictable factor and some of the larger cars began to break essential components early in the race, including a big Bugatti, which spun round in uncontrollable circles when its torque tube broke.

During the first part of the race the Wisdoms' Riley held on to fifth place, with both drivers lapping at about the same speed. In the second half another Bugatti broke its steering, the engines of three more cars began making very expensive noises and several drivers found that they were having to cope without any brakes. Cars were scattered all over the circuit, with their drivers and mechanics frantically trying to carry out repairs. By the end of the race only nine out of the 37 original starters were still running, with the Wisdoms' Riley among them and finishing in fourth place.

They drove at Le Mans again that year, but both were forced to retire, Bill with her Riley and Tommy in his Singer. The teams were staying at different hotels and Bill decided to book out of the hotel she had been staying in with the Riley team and go back with Tommy to his hotel, so that they could get a good night's sleep and leave early for home the following morning. When the French chambermaid brought them breakfast Bill's half-hearted attempt to explain that the man next to her in the bed really was her husband was met with a wry smile and to Bill's embarrassment the maid still had an amused expression on her face as she closed the door quietly behind her.

The Wisdoms went next to the Craigantlet Hill Climb in Ireland, where they put up identical times in the Frazer-Nash, then in 1936 Bill drove a Fiat in the Tourist Trophy Race at the Ards circuit, just outside Belfast. Unfortunately, the engine of the Fiat packed up after about an hour, but she described driving round such a glorious circuit even for a short time as being a most memorable experience.

In 1937 Tommy and Bill decided to drive a works MG together in the famous Mille Miglia, the 1,000-mile road race round Italy now banned as being too dangerous. The race started and finished at Brescia and went through Verona, Ancona, Pescara, Rome, Siena, Florence, Bologna, Piacenza and Mantua. It always seemed that every Italian driver who could get hold of a really fast car was determined to take part.

The cars were sent off at regular intervals, with both drivers having to remain in the car throughout the 1,000 miles, so that one could navigate or rest while the other drove, until it was time to change over. The Italian crowds who lined most of the route made it more dangerous for the drivers by insisting on straying on to the road while the race was still in progress. In trying to miss a woman who had stepped in front of their car, Tommy slewed the MG hard round, but it spun off the road, cannoning off one tree and into another, and Bill, who was thrown through the windscreen, was knocked unconscious and suffered serious facial injuries. As Tommy had a broken leg, they were both rushed to a hospital nearby and Bill woke up to find her face covered in bandages. Tommy's broken leg healed quite quickly, but Bill had to undergo months of painful plastic surgery before she was fit enough to race again.

Although several of their friends tried to persuade them to give up racing, there was little chance of that, and Bill was at Le Mans again in 1938, driving an MG belonging to Dorothy Stanley-Turner, who had come second in her class with it the previous year. Dorothy was still suffering from the after effects of diphtheria and was in no state to drive, so she asked Bill to take her place with Arthur Dobson as her co-driver.

He was also unwell, and the MG had to have a rather hurried preparation. From the start the car didn't seem to be going as fast as it should, but it was still lapping fast enough to stand a chance of a class win when the clutch started to slip. Liberal applications of fire-extinguisher fluid cured the problem for a while, but when it started again and the engine began to sound really rough there was no option but to withdraw the MG after 48 laps.

The war virtually brought to an end Bill's motor racing career. Tommy joined the Royal Air Force and reached the rank of wing commander, but when the war ended and he returned to civvy street the racing scene was very different. Brooklands had gone and what little circuit racing there was took place mainly on former airfields such as Silverstone. With nowhere suitable for her to race, Bill turned to rallies and hill climbs and took part in both with considerable success. Tommy raced sports cars, particularly Aston Martins, Jaguars and Healeys, but he also competed in international rallies, sometimes with Bill as his co-driver.

In 1951 they were driving together in the Alpine Rally, when their Bristol was involved in a collision while they were taking part in a high-speed run round the Cortina circuit. The organisers had taken the usual steps to ensure that the circuit was closed to all other traffic, but the driver of a large American car, after removing the safety barrier that had been placed across the entrance, drove straight on to the circuit and met Tommy and Bill's Bristol coming the other way. There was the inevitable head-on collision and the Wisdoms, who were both injured, were taken to a makeshift hospital near to the circuit, which used to be the local workhouse. When Bill regained consciousness she thought there was something strange about the place and asked Tommy, who was in the adjoining bed, where they were.

'In the workhouse!' said Tommy, with his usual sense of humour.

'What already?' replied Bill. 'I always knew we would end up here sooner or later, but I didn't think it would be quite so soon.'

Her sudden death on 13 April 1972, at the age of 68, deprived the racing world of a very remarkable woman, highly talented, shrewd and extremely brave. Some critics felt that she was the most outstanding of all the prewar women drivers, but, whether or not that was the case, she was certainly one of the best.

15

The Darling of the Brooklands Crowds

Since the famous Blue Bird café at Brooklands was burned down in 1917, the Aero Club bar had become the favourite haunt of most of the pilots, and the usual noisy crowd of members and their friends were there when Henry Petre walked in one Saturday afternoon in 1930, accompanied by a stunningly beautiful brunette, whom he introduced as his wife. It was not the woman's film-star looks that were such a surprise and set tongues wagging, but the news that Henry Petre was married.

His fellow fliers had nicknamed him 'Peter the Monk' and were convinced that he had taken a vow of celibacy, because he didn't seem to have any interest in women. It seemed strange to them that, whenever an attractive girl joined their party, he would always make some excuse and take off in his rather crude Deperdussin monoplane, then circle the airfield until he thought the coast was clear. The news that he was now married, and to such a very bubbly and vivacious young Canadian girl, had come as rather a shock.

Although Henry Petre was a wealthy and successful London solicitor, he was also quite a shy man and it was true that he did feel rather embarrassed in the company of women, but Kay Defries was different. Henry had met her while on one of his regular visits to Canada for the winter sports, and it had been love at first sight. As luck would have it Kay had also fallen in love with the tall, handsome Englishman and found his shyness rather refreshing, after the rather boisterous behaviour of her brothers' friends and most of the other men she had met.

She was a member of a wealthy and very sporting Toronto family and, in addition to being a brilliant ice skater, Kay had been brought up to be fiercely competitive in everything she did, which became very evident when she began racing cars. Henry had never met anyone quite like her and, having plucked up enough courage to ask her to marry him, he couldn't believe his luck when she not only accepted but also agreed to leave Canada and the winter sports she enjoyed so much and return to England with him.

Although they had many interests in common, Kay didn't share Henry's passion for flying, but, as he and his brother were both pioneer pilots and had been flying from Brooklands for several years, she didn't want to do anything to spoil her husband's obvious enjoyment of the sport. It was while Henry was off flying with some of his friends one weekend that she wandered over to the Brooklands circuit and saw her first motor race. She spent the Saturday afternoon soaking up the atmosphere and in between races going along to the pits to meet some of the drivers and see their cars at close quarters. By the end of the afternoon Kay knew what she wanted to do. As she was married to a flier, she saw no reason why she couldn't become a racing driver and told her husband so over dinner that evening.

Henry hoped at first that motor racing might be just a passing interest on his wife's part, but that was obviously not going to be the case, when the following weekend she asked whether he would allow her to drive his much-loved 4.5-litre Invicta in one of the women's races. He had no intention of allowing that to happen, but it was a ploy that worked, and Kay was delighted when Henry bought her a red Wolseley Hornet Daytona Special from Eustace Watkins for her birthday and persuaded his friend, the great L G Hornsted, who had more experience of racing at Brooklands than anyone else he knew, to teach her how to drive it properly.

With his help it didn't take Kay long to learn how to cope with Brooklands' difficult track conditions, including the bumps that could unexpectedly launch a car and driver into the air, some-times with dire results. Hornsted also taught her the correct line to take when overtaking and why it was inadvisable to go too high on the banking unless the weight and speed of the car warranted it.

After such excellent tuition it was not surprising that Kay was placed third and second in her first two races with the Wolseley, but she knew she still had a lot to learn, and persuaded some of the top drivers, who seemed flattered to be asked for help by such an attractive young woman, to let her do a few laps of the circuit in their machines during the practice sessions. In this way she gained invaluable experience of handling different types of racing cars very quickly, but, because she was so petite and some of the other drivers were rather large, she had to have a special collapsible seat made, which fitted into the cockpit of each of the cars she was driving and enabled her to reach the pedals more easily and see over the steering wheel properly.

Although she went on to win several races with her red

Wolseley Special, Kay's racing career really took off in 1933, when Henry bought her a second-hand supercharged 2-litre Grand Prix Bugatti for £150. She at last had a proper racing car of her own to drive, and although it could be temperamental at times, which no doubt accounted for its low price, the Bugatti proved to be a fine schoolmaster and taught her how to cope with some of the much faster and more powerful cars she was to race later.

Her methodical approach to everything she did was one of the reasons why Kay's motor-racing career progressed so rapidly. She was also a good listener and a quick learner, and was determined to find out all she could about the sport. She had the Bugatti repainted a lighter shade of French blue, to match her overalls, and made sure it was maintained in showroom condition by George Boyle, who was employed by Papworth, a well-known character in the racing world who specialised in the marque.

Although Kay was never afraid to get her hands dirty and ignored all the usual dirt and oil associated with motor racing, she always arrived at the start with her car looking immaculate. The lipstick and powder puff she kept handy in the cockpit also enabled her to repair her make-up at the end of each race, before returning to the paddock to face all the photographers.

During the following five years Kay appeared at nearly every Brooklands meeting driving a variety of cars. At the autumn meeting in 1933 she entered her Bugatti in the first ladies' handicap to be run over the Mountain Circuit, with its famous fork hairpin and climbing turn on to the Members' Banking from the finishing straight. The course called for a combination of cool nerves and skilful driving and the officials were still not convinced that women drivers would be up to the task. They decided to let the race go ahead, however, and, not surprisingly, there was no shortage of entries, from Whitney Straight's MG Magnette, driven by the London dancer Psyche Altham, to Freddie Dixon's very fast black Riley 9, driven by his sister Rita Don.

Freddie Dixon had had a substantial bet with one of the bookmakers at Brooklands that the Riley would win the race, but he became rather concerned during practice about his sister's habit of lifting her foot off the accelerator too soon going into the corners. She was far too cautious for his liking and to ensure this didn't happen during the race he arranged to travel as her riding mechanic, which was allowed under the rules.

According to Sammy Davis, a close friend of Freddie Dixon, who met him in the bar after the race, Rita had been given some sharp encouragement to go faster by her brother, which was not strictly according to the rules. Before going to the start Freddie had tied a piece of string to the Riley's throttle and fixed the other end to a ring he'd placed beside him in the cockpit. He'd also armed himself with a long hatpin.

Every time during the race that his sister looked like braking too quickly, Freddie gave her a quick jab with the pin and pulled sharply on the string to open up the throttle. If some of the spectators were puzzled by the rather erratic way in which the Riley sometimes slowed down going into a corner, then suddenly shot forward again with the driver leaping in the air, they probably put it down to the usual bumps on the track.

As Freddie had predicted, although Kay Petre had been the favourite to take the race, it was the Riley that won at a very respectable 62.68 m.p.h., finishing 5.2 seconds ahead of Kay's Bugatti. Although Rita was seen having a furious argument with her brother after the race, there was nothing she could do. Freddie had won his bet and as soon as the Riley was back in the paddock he'd removed the string and disposed of the hatpin, which were the only two pieces of incriminating evidence.

The 1934 season was a particularly good one for Kay and she began to show her true potential with some outstanding drives, mainly in cars lent to her by Thomas Fotheringham, Oliver Bertram and Dick Shuttleworth. It speaks volumes for Kay's ability and charm that they were prepared to trust such valuable cars to a woman driver with only limited racing experience.

After she'd taken Dick Shuttleworth's 2.3-litre Bugatti round the Brooklands Outer Circuit at 117.74 m.p.h., despite having trouble with the plugs, it was her handling of the huge twelve-cylinder, 10.5-litre Delage, usually driven by Oliver Bertram, that caught everyone's attention and gave a clear indication of her undoubted skill and nerve. The car's normal seat had been replaced by one specially built to fit Kay's tiny, trim figure, and the enormous size of the Delage only emphasised just how small she looked in her pale-blue overalls and helmet and neat, flat-heeled shoes.

The spectators rushed across to watch and there was a real sense of expectation as, after a few warm-up laps to get used to the car, Kay put in a scintillatingly fast lap of 129.58 m.p.h. to create a new women's lap record. She had succeeded in doing so despite a treacherous crosswind, which was also very gusty and made the conditions even worse.

As a result of that performance, Kay was presented with one of the coveted 120 m.p.h. Brooklands badges and there was a lot less talk from the officials and the other drivers about allowing women to handle very big, fast cars. Kay was such a slim and petite person that it was remarkable how she managed to stay in the cockpit of the Delage as it went over the famous Brooklands bumps at high speed, and when she climbed from the car the paddock commentators wanted to know how she managed to control such a huge beast.

Kay's only explanation was that she believed a woman should always sit close to the wheel so that she could make full use of her shoulders to reinforce the strength of her arms. Whatever the method she used, it certainly worked with her.

16

The Battle for the Wakefield Cup

Kay Petre's first experience of being a member of a racing team came in 1934 during the Light Car Club's Relay Race at Brooklands, which was always one of the most popular events of the season. That year's race was a memorable occasion, not only because Kay's team of works Singers won the Wakefield Cup for the best performance by a women's team on a technicality – which should never have been included in the rules – but because most of the top women drivers were competing for the cup and they proved just how tough they were. They were all determined to win, despite having to race under terrible weather conditions. Sammy Davis described being manager of the Singer team as a very rewarding experience, with all the women driving immaculately to his instructions throughout the race and showing remarkable resolution and courage despite the atrocious weather.

In addition to Kay, the Singer team consisted of Mrs Tolhurst and Eileen Ellison, and they were up against fierce competition from the team of works MGs under the benign eye of Captain George Eyston. The team's captain was Irene Schwedler and the other two drivers were Margaret Allan and Doreen Evans. Cecil Kimber, the dynamic head of the MG Company, had made it known that if they won the Ladies' Cup he would enter them as an all-woman team in the 24-hour race at Le Mans. He knew that their main threat could come from the Singer team, but he didn't realise that there hadn't been sufficient time for all their cars to be prepared properly. Sammy Davis was particularly worried about the performance of the slowest of the three Singers, to be driven by Eileen Ellison.

The organisers had instigated a rule that during practice all the drivers had to cover three laps watched by an official observer, then come into the pits and hand the sash over to the next member of the team, as they would do in the race. When it was the turn of the Singer team to do their compulsory practice laps under scrutiny, the official observer made the mistake of slipping away to the tea tent for a hot drink and something to eat.

Seeing what had happened, Kay Petre followed him into the tent and dragged him back to the Singer pits. He looked very red-faced, with tea spilled down the front of his coat and holding a half-eaten sticky bun. He was apologising profusely to Kay, who was trying hard to keep a straight face and managed to do so until they reached the pits, where she and the rest of the team burst into fits of laughter.

All the women took the race very seriously, and George Eyston gave each member of the MG team a set of confidential instructions regarding running order, lap speeds, pit signals, refuelling times and other information relating to the team's overall racing strategy. Everyone had been told to learn the instructions off by heart, so that on the day of the race everything should run smoothly. That might have been the case if one of the girls hadn't left her copy of the instructions lying on the pit counter just as the race was about to begin and a gust of wind blew them into the pits allocated to the Singer team.

It was Kay Petre who noticed them lying on the ground and handed them to Sammy Davis, who immediately placed one of his assistants in a position down the course where he could see all the MG team's pit signals as soon as they appeared. Throughout the race he was able to relay them back to the Singer pits so that Sammy could look up what each signal meant and instruct his drivers accordingly. The knowledge that they were aware of all their rival's race plans was a great confidence booster to the Singer team, and the members of the MG team couldn't understand why, throughout the race, Kay and her colleagues seemed to be sharing some huge joke at their expense.

Irene Schwedler was the first away for the MG team and averaged a steady 90 m.p.h. for lap after lap, causing considerable concern to all the other teams. The much-vaunted Austin works team were eliminated early on, when their leading car was forced to stop out on the circuit and the driver broke the rules by taking a short cut back to the pits across the infield, before handing over the sash to the next member of the team.

After completing her scheduled thirty laps, Irene Schwedler handed the sash to Margaret Allan, who ran like a hare to her car, started the engine and was smartly away with an expression of grim determination on her face. Her lap speeds were even faster than Irene's, but she couldn't understand why, as soon as she was given orders to speed up or slow down, the Singer driver sticking grimly to her tail did exactly the same.

Sammy Davis's team, meanwhile were already having their share of troubles. However hard she tried, Eileen Ellison, who had taken over after the first thirty laps, hadn't been able to make her car go fast enough. He was still debating whether to call her in and send Kay off in the third car, when a jet of scalding steam shot from the Singer's radiator on to Eileen's hands and face. She managed to keep control of the car and, despite being dripping wet and in considerable discomfort, she coasted back to the pits to hand the sash over to Kay Petre. Her courage and presence of mind saved the team valuable minutes, because, if she had stopped her car out on the circuit, Kay would have had to waste valuable time running round the track to get the sash.

Now with little time lost she was able to stay close to Margaret's MG, despite a further deterioration in the weather, which had worsened all day. A cloudburst meant that the cars had to go through solid sheets of water and the track began to look more like a lake. Although this had the advantage of slowing some of the faster cars, it made conditions very dangerous for all the competitors. One car spun several times in the wet, missing the scorer's box by a whisper, then slid wildly along tail first before crashing into the barrier by the competitors' car park.

The driver of a car that had been sitting on the tail of Kay's Singer, hoping to be towed along in the slipstream, became blinded by the additional streams of spray and to Kay's delight was forced to slow down and stop annoying her. Conditions became so bad that several competitors just gave up and one came into the pits, called for a large umbrella and sat underneath it smoking a cigarette, refusing to get back into his car until the weather improved. Kay came into the pits for a visor, after finding that her goggles were useless in the heavy rain, but it was immediately blown off by the blustery wind and she had to do the best she could with the goggles.

There was consternation in the Singer pits shortly afterwards when there was no sign of her or the car, and the other members of the team began to fear the worst; but their concern turned to relief some minutes later when the Singer appeared travelling very slowly. After crawling into the pits, Kay explained that the throttle had come adrift and she had been forced to stop by the side of the track to carry out running repairs. She was drenched to the skin, obviously very cold, and seemed in no condition to continue, but insisted that, while there was still a chance of their winning the Wakefield Cup, there was no question of her pulling out of the race. While the mechanics were working frantically to repair the broken throttle, a few pits away a driver was standing ankle deep in mud, trying to change his car's plugs, which had become waterlogged.

The unscheduled pitstop had caused the Singer team to drop a few places and the chances of them now finishing ahead of the MGs, who were lying in third place, seemed rather remote; but the girls were relieved when Sammy Davis explained that the rules stated that the Wakefield Cup could not be won by any team finishing in the first three places overall. The MG team obviously didn't know this and continued going flat out.

They were delayed slightly when Margaret Allan had a narrow escape because a tyre tread had come off when she was travelling at close on 100 m.p.h. There was a loud bang and bits of rubber shot in all directions, several of them hitting her arm and causing the car to skid across the track as though it had met a bad patch of ice. She kept her head and managed to reach the pits with a stream of sparks flying from the bare wheel rim as it made contact with the ground. Doreen Evans took over the sash and, without any instructions from her pit to slow down, remained in third place.

After rejoining the race, Kay had hardly been visible through all the spray coming up from her car, but she had continued going for lap after lap as regularly as clockwork, and steadily made up the lost time. Keeping an accurate check on the number of laps each car had completed became very difficult, because the lap charts had been reduced to a soggy mess by the rain, but there was some light relief for the spectators when one soaking-wet driver stopped by the Singer pits, leaped from the cockpit of his car, removed his soggy shoes and emptied the water from them, then took off his socks and carefully wrung them out one at a time, then put them on again and rejoined the race.

The MG team had done brilliantly to finish third overall, having averaged 82.66 m.p.h. for the race, but the coveted Wakefield Cup still went to the Singer team, who finish in fifth place. It was also a victory for Sammy Davis, who had studied the rules more carefully than George Eyston.

Kay Petre's most outstanding achievement during the 1934 season was being invited to be a member of the successful Riley works team at Le Mans and to partner Dorothy Champney, the very talented driver who later married Victor Riley. The other members of the team that year were Von der Becke, Peacock, Newsome and Percy Maclure, while the three other Rileys were driven by Freddy Dixon with Cyril Paul, Jean Sebilleau with Georges Delaroche and Jean Trevoux with René Carriere.

The race began with a battle for the lead between the large Alfa Romeos and the Bugattis at speeds that were impossible to maintain for the full 24 hours. By the halfway stage, they were all in trouble and the Aston Martins and Rileys began to come into their own. As daylight broke, the car driven by Kay and Dorothy was lying in fourteenth place and the disappearance of the Aston Martins with engine trouble had improved the Riley team's chances very considerably. When the race ended, they had achieved what they set out to do and were the winners of the coveted Rudge-Whitworth Cup, finishing with all six cars intact. Kay and Dorothy had ended in eleventh place, averaging more than 60 m.p.h. for the full 24 hours, which was a very good performance for a 1.5-litre car.

17

Kay Petre Takes the Fastest-Woman Title

The 1935 season began on a high note for Kay Petre, when she lapped Brooklands at 127.38 m.p.h. in the big 10.7-litre V12 Delage, which had been adapted for her to race regularly by extending the pedals and installing a special seat in the cockpit to enable her to see better. It was the car that in 1924 had set a new land-speed record of 143 m.p.h. on the bumpy Arpajon stretch of road near Paris. In 1935 she also won a very fast handicap race on the Brooklands Outer Circuit in Dick Shuttleworth's Bugatti at 118 m.p.h., having put in the fastest lap of 125.48 m.p.h., and bought the famous 1.5-litre supercharged 'White' Riley from Raymond Mays and had it resprayed in her favourite 'Petrol Blue' to match her racing overalls.

The Riley was to prove a very successful purchase, and, having taken third place with it in a Brooklands mountain race, she then broke the Class F lap record at 77.97 m.p.h. At the Whitsun meeting she also managed a third place in the Delage, despite being baulked by smaller cars travelling too high on the bankings, which meant she repeatedly had to drive below them to overtake in the best tradition of J G Parry Thomas and some of the other great masters of the Brooklands circuit.

The highlight of her year, however, was undoubtedly the challenge match she had with Gwenda Hawkes. It was promoted as the race to find out which of the two was the faster driver and entitled to be called 'The Brooklands Speed Queen'. Kay didn't like the title or all the hype, but accepted that it was probably good for motor racing and women drivers and in any case there was little she could do about it. Brooklands had arranged the challenge and was also responsible for all the publicity.

Gwenda arrived from Paris with her very potent 1.6-litre supercharged Derby-Miller, which held the outright track record at Montlhery. Her husband Douglas had done his best to modify the decidedly temperamental car, to make it better suited to the different conditions at Brooklands, and had fitted a specially designed silencer, which was needed because of the Surrey track's noise regulations. Kay chose to drive the considerably older 10.7-litre Delage, which had been built in 1924 and was the fastest car available to her.

The race officials very quickly got cold feet during the first practice session, when Gwenda put in a lap of 130 m.p.h. to record the fastest lap at Brooklands by a woman, until Kay went round soon afterwards at 134.75 m.p.h. It was clear that both women were determined to win the title, even if it meant driving their cars to the absolute limit, and there had never been a race run there at anything like those speeds. The very worried officials held a hurried conference and decided that allowing the two women to race against each other would be courting disaster, but as a compromise agreed that each driver should do three timed circuits of the track and the one recording the fastest lap would be the winner.

Both women agreed and the crowd waited in an atmosphere of hushed anticipation as the Delage was pushed to the starting line and the diminutive figure of Kay Petre eased herself into the cockpit. The powerful engine roared into life and as the starter's flag fell the Delage shot off down the straight and, despite a slipping clutch, recorded a standing lap of 129.03 m.p.h. A lap of 134.24 m.p.h. followed and the final lap was slightly less spectacular at 132.88 m.p.h. Only nine drivers had ever attained such speeds on the circuit.

Gwenda then arrived on the starting line with the long, low Derby-Miller. The car's acceleration and overall performance was really remarkable and Gwenda had just done a lap of 133.67 m.p.h. when the silencer exploded and the cockpit was filled with fumes, forcing her to retire. Kay consequently won the contest and was awarded the title, but the following day Gwenda tried again after repairs had been made to the silencer and did a lap of 135.95 m.p.h., which remains the fastest lap ever recorded by a woman at Brooklands.

Kay and Gwenda were both awarded their Brooklands 130-m.p.h. badges and became the only two women among the very few men to receive them. Even those who still had reservations about women drivers had to admit that Kay's lap of 134.24 m.p.h. and Gwenda's of 135.95 m.p.h. were two of the finest performances seen at the track. Several commentators claimed afterwards that, had the two women been allowed to race against each other, Kay would certainly have won, because of her greater knowledge and experience of circuit racing, but she rejected the suggestion. Kay also denied that before the event she had shown Gwenda round Brooklands and given her hints on how to handle the track.

'Gwenda is such a brilliant driver, that would certainly not have been necessary,' she said, adding 'She is perfectly capable of driving any car very fast on any circuit, including at Brooklands.'

Kay drove at Le Mans again in 1935 as a member of the Riley works team and her partner on that occasion was her close friend and rival Bill Wisdom. Once again there were six cars in the team, the others being driven by Von der Becke and Richardson, Freddie Dixon and Cyril Paul, Sebilleau and Delaroche, Percy Maclure and Newsome, and Jean Trevoux and René Carriere. There was heavy rain for most of the race and after their fine performances the previous year the Riley drivers were out of luck. Kay and Bill Wisdom were forced to retire on lap 38, when an engine bearing went; Freddie Dixon's Riley caught fire; Delaroche's car skidded badly and crashed, leaving Von der Becke to finish fourth and Trevoux fifth.

In 1936 Kay drove an ERA in the International Trophy Race at Brooklands, which was the long-distance simulated road event held there. The car not only suffered from bouts of misfiring, but her race ended when the ERA spun into the chicane at the famous Fork Turn and she was unable to restart the engine. She ran back to the pits for help, furious with herself and covered with sand, but the incident with the chicane had lost her any chance she had of winning. Kay always maintained that she disliked the ERA more than any other car, probably with good reason.

In the Brooklands Racing Club's '500' race on the Outer Circuit that year, her Riley was also plagued with valve gear problems, but everything came right for her at the closing meeting of the season when she won the Mountain race outright, sliding through the corners with her Riley in terrific style and beating all the men over the very tricky course.

The following year she took a works 1.5-litre Riley to South Africa for the Grand Prix, but the correct fuel for the highly tuned engine didn't arrive in time and she could do no better than finish eleventh. The visit was a memorable one for her, however, because she was allowed to drive one of the very fast rear-engined, 6-litre, 16-cyclinder Grand Prix Auto Unions. Apart from Elly Beinhorn, who was Bernard Rosemeyer's wife, she was the only woman ever allowed to drive one of the famous German team cars and described the experience as being 'just wonderful'. After the race the German team manager presented her with a signed photograph showing her with the car and with Von Delius and Rosemeyer towering over her. It remained one of her most treasured possessions.

Kay raced many times at Donington Park, which was as near to a real road-racing circuit in Britain as it was possible to get on private land, but it was a particularly difficult circuit for drivers because it measured only two miles round and contained so many different types of corner. In 1936 she looked like being involved in a nasty accident there when an oil line broke on her Riley, showering her with hot oil. Seemingly unperturbed by what had happened, she coasted round to the pits, grabbed an overcoat she saw lying on the pit counter, then, finding a clean pair of overalls, she used the coat as a tent, did a quick-change act while the mechanics were making the necessary repairs and then, to the obvious delight of the spectators, she roared back into the race. No wonder the crowds loved her.

18

Two Men and a Girl

The peak of Kay Petre's remarkable racing career came in 1937 when she was invited to join the famous Austin works team of single-seater cars. She was given a 750cc side-valve model to drive, while Charles Goodacre and Bert Hadley had the two twin-overhead-camshaft cars. Kay described her time with the Austin team as her happiest period since she began racing. She liked the cars, her fellow drivers and the mechanics, whom she described as being 'absolutely first-class'. While they were away 'on tour', as she put it, they all lived together as a team and there was always a terrific spirit wherever they were.

It rained throughout the whole of the 1937 Empire Trophy Race at Donington Park and with the smaller-engined cars starting first, Charles Dodson led the way with the first of the Austins, closely followed by Percy Maclure with a Riley and then Kay, who seemed to look smaller than ever.

Each car left a wave of spray behind it, which made overtaking particularly difficult, and to add to Kay's troubles the throttle of her Austin began to stick open, making the situation even more dangerous. Some frantic work in the pits by the mechanics seemed to have cured the problem, but soon after she got going again it became clear that there was something else seriously wrong, because the engine was not responding properly to any throttle movement.

A lap later the engine cut out completely and there was a strong smell of petrol, which suggested there would be a likelihood of fire if she didn't take immediate action. Kay pulled off the track, but the worried mechanics who rushed to the car could not find the trouble and she was forced to retire. When the carburettor was stripped down later, the cause of all the trouble was found to be a jet needle which had broken in half, something that had never happened to any of their cars before.

It was certainly not the Austin team's day. Coming in to refuel, Charles Dobson asked if he should switch off the engine, but before he could do so the mechanics had already filled the petrol tank to overflowing. As he switched off there was a flash at the end of the tailpipe and a loud 'whoosh' as the car went up in flames. The mechanics managed to get Charles out of the cockpit, but not before he had been badly burned. It took the firemen some time to extinguish the flaming car, by which time it was completely gutted.

The Coronation 100-mile race over the same circuit brought better results for the team, with Charles Goodacre taking the lead soon after the start, followed by Kay, who had got away better than Bert Hadley, but he had the faster overhead-valve car and took second place on the next lap, only to be overtaken by the popular Pat Fairfield in an ERA. Although Hadley was in trouble later, the Austin team were not to be denied victory. Charles Goodacre won easily, with Charles Martin's big Alfa second, Gee's Riley third, Kenneth Evans's Alfa fourth and Kay fifth with the slower side-valve Austin. Hadley had better luck during the team's next visit to Donington, coming home first with Goodacre second and Kay again fifth.

In the important Nuffield Trophy Race later that year, the Austin team were lying first, second and third, when Bert Hadley had to retire with his engine misfiring badly and Kay's car fractured an oil pipe when she was lying in second place. The cockpit became flooded with oil, scalding one of her legs, and officials in the Austin pit feared the worst when there was no news of her, until some minutes later she coasted into view with one leg dangling over the side of the cockpit. Her blue racing overalls were green with the hot oil, which seemed to be everywhere, even over the steering wheel, the pedals and the tail of the car.

After borrowing Marjorie Eccles's top coat and a towel, she disappeared to the back of the pits and, after wriggling out of her oil-soaked overalls, replaced them with a pair belonging to one of the men. She emerged some time later looking cleaner and wearing overalls three sizes too big for her. Then, to everyone's amusement, she trotted happily about in them for the remainder of the race.

After the team's troubles at Donington the Relay Race at Brooklands came as a welcome relief. Bert Hadley set off to do the first thirty laps at a speed that was very near to the record for the class, then handed over to Goodacre in the second car. By the time he had completed his thirty laps the team were well up with their rivals. Kay took over in the side-valve car and after a cautious start went like a scalded cat, catching the leaders with every lap. Even being sprayed with oil from the reserve tank didn't slow her down and the Austin team went on to win the race at 105.63 m.p.h. The high average speed was all the more remarkable because, unlike the sports cars, the single-seater

Austins did not have self-starters and each car had to be push-started, which took up valuable time.

The twelve-hour race at Donington was more like a shortened version of the 24-hour race at Le Mans, with two members of the team allotted to each car and the drivers taking turns to drive. Bert Hadley was teamed up with Charles Dobson, Charles Goodacre with Buckley, while Kay had as her co-driver a young works apprentice called Stephenson, who did drive well but was unfortunately very much taller. Every time Kay took over from him, she had to reupholster the seat using a combined cushion and back rest designed specially for her.

At the halfway stage the rain came down in torrents, making conditions difficult for all the drivers, who were soon soaked to the skin and blinded by the spray from the cars in front. Such treacherous conditions made overtaking even more dangerous, and there was a bad accident when Billing, driving an AC, went through Red Gate turn on the tail of Robinson's Riley. Both cars slid on the wet road, collided and crashed into a stone wall. The race was almost brought to a standstill while the wreckage was cleared away sufficiently to allow the other cars to pass. The hold-up, which enabled some of the cars that had been overtaken to catch up, probably deprived Austin of the team prize, which they lost to MG only during the last lap. In the end, Hadley and Dobson's Austin came second, with Goodacre and Buckley third and Kay and Stephenson finishing a creditable fifth, having covered 602.27 miles during the twelve hours.

Towards the end of the race the Austin team manager, realising that Kay was being sprayed with hot oil and remembering how she had been scalded in similar circumstances at Donington, debated whether to call her in, but decided against it when the other team members impressed on him that Kay would signal if she found the situation to be more than she could stand, and was certainly tough enough to last out the race.

Apart from driving the Austin company's single-seater racing cars, Kay was also chosen to drive for them in sports-car races that year, including at Le Mans, where Charles Goodacre and Dennis Buckley drove the first car, Charles Dobson and Bert Hadley the second and Kay and Mangan the third. Fifty-eight cars faced the starter, but within an hour there was chaos. One of the big Bugattis, which during the first eight laps had seemed to be very unsteady going into White House, attempted to overtake a car that had strayed from its correct line as it went into the famous curve.

The Bugatti skidded and, after hitting the bank, turned broadside to the road and was rammed by a big Delahaye travelling very fast. A French Talbot then came round the corner and crashed into the tangle of cars, adding to the wreckage, which by then almost blocked the road. That was the moment when the immensely popular driver Pat Fairfield tragically arrived on the scene and his Frazer-Nash spun out of control. He'd been hampered by a Riley, whose driver, seeing the situation, could do nothing but jam on his brakes and go into a skid. Pat was thrown out over the steering wheel when his car collided with the bank and, although he stood there for a while looking dazed, but apparently uninjured, he collapsed and died later from serious internal injuries.

After the accident the pace of the race slowed for a while, but the situation was made much worse by one of the torrential thunderstorms for which Le Mans is famous. Nobody could see the road properly through all the rain, and a Delahaye skidded into the sand at one of the turns and had to be dug out. Wimille, who was driving the leading Bugatti with Benoist, swerved so vigorously to avoid another car that he only just avoided colliding with the pits. Then disaster overtook the whole of the Austin team.

Charles Goodacre arrived at the pits in an exhausted state, having run all the way there after abandoning his broken-down car out on the circuit when he was unable to push it any further. He reported that there was something wrong with the Austin's fuel supply and his co-driver, Dennis Buckley, was sent to see what he could do, but he was unable to fix the trouble and they were forced to retire their car, having covered only 32 laps. When Dobson's car was also forced to retire after 74 laps and Kay's after 72 laps, both with bearing trouble, the Austin challenge for that year was at an end.

The Le Mans regulations strictly forbade drivers from carrying spares in their cars and anyone caught doing so was liable to get instant disqualification. If the guilty person was a woman, however, French chivalry sometimes resulted in a little rule bending. During the 1937 race one of the French pit officials asked Sammy Davis whether he thought that English girls were as physically attractive as French girls?

'I don't think there, is much to choose between them,' replied Sammy, with his usual tact.

The Frenchman then pointed to Kay Petre, who was standing at the next pit counter waiting for her car to come in for a change of drivers, and said, 'Now there's a lovely girl and what a wonderful figure, but don't you think her ankles could be prettier, or are your English girls built rather differently from ours?'

Sammy looked down at Kay's ankles and there in the leg of her overalls was the unmistakable outline of a gasket. It was the official's duty to report the fact, but all he did was smile and say, 'The poor girl. Without doubt she has had a serious accident. She has my sympathy, but let's hope that whatever is causing her to have such an ugly-shaped ankle will disappear in due course.'

If Kay's car needed some vital part to keep it going, she was quite up to stuffing the spare down the leg of her racing overalls under the nose of the officials. A man probably wouldn't have got away with it, but Kay always had a way with officials.

She was certainly very versatile and was as effective driving in hill climbs as she was on a racing circuit. In 1937, driving her favourite supercharged single-seater Austin, she finally settled who was the fastest woman to drive up the famous Shelsley Walsh hill, in Worcestershire, Britain's most historic hill climb. The short, steep hill has always been very difficult to take at high speed and few drivers managed to get every aspect of it right. Most of the cars usually had all four wheels in the air at one stage or another and fractions of seconds gained or lost on a curve or corner can mean the difference between success and failure. Getting a car away from the starting line quickly involves controlling wheel spin and rapid acceleration, so that the use of the throttle and the clutch always needs to be carefully judged.

The women's record received particular prominence that year, because all the top drivers decided to have a go at lowering it. Slim and attractive Barbara Skinner, her long black hair coiled tightly round her head under a smart driving helmet, had gone up the hill in 46.6 seconds in her Morris special. Eileen Ellison's Maserati was not really suited to the hill and the Australian Joan Richmond's HRG was not fast enough. Dorothy Stanley-Turner sensibly bided her time with her Q-type MG, until she had mastered all the hill's complexities, while Doreen Evans drove her R-type MG with great enterprise, but the engine was misfiring and she registered a disappointing 46.4 seconds. Bill Wisdom then went up in 48 seconds in an Austin, which did not sound at all happy, to be followed by Kay, who tore up the hill in 45.2 seconds with her supercharged Austin. When Doreen Evans's next climb took only 44.8 seconds, despite her brother's plea to 'be careful', Kay put everything into her next run and managed to equal her time.

The crowd lining the hill had been watching the battle with increasing interest, but there were now those who wanted the contest called off in case one of the drivers got injured. Kay and Doreen insisted on a final run up the hill, however, in order to settle the issue. Kay went first and reduced her time for the climb to 43.8 seconds, at which point Doreen's car decided, perhaps fortuitously, but much to its owner's fury, that it had had enough, and the record went to Kay.

19

A Tragic End to a Brilliant and Colourful Racing Career

Kay Petre's successful career as a racing driver came to a sad and untimely end in September 1937, when she was at Brooklands practising for the British Racing Drivers' Club's popular 500-mile race. Tragedy struck while she was travelling round the Byfleet banking in her single-seater Austin and holding a steady course about halfway up the slope. Just before the Byfleet Bridge and without any warning, Reg Parnell's MG suddenly stalled on the banking above her and slewed violently sideways and downwards out of control, before striking the tail of Kay's car and rolling it over and over down the banking.

Many drivers would probably not have survived such a horrific accident, but Kay's determination pulled her through, although she had serious head injuries and for days her life hung in the balance. Her condition gradually improved until she was well enough to withstand several sessions of painful plastic surgery. In time her partial paralysis also disappeared, although she was left with permanent damage to some muscles down one side of her face.

Reg Parnell had his competition licence taken away, but it was largely due to Kay's intervention he got it back again after twelve months. To show there were no hard feelings on her part, she insisted on being on the starting grid at Brooklands for his first race after regaining his licence and to wish him a successful return to racing. After the war Reg Parnell became a popular and successful Grand Prix driver and he and Kay remained good friends. Kay was always very philosophical about the accident that so nearly ended her life and refused to discuss it, except to say. 'If you race fast cars, one of the risks you take is that one day you might cop it!'

Although Kay knew that the accident had virtually brought to an end her successful racing career, she was determined to prove that she hadn't lost her nerve. On 23 March 1938 she did race again and to the delight of the large crowd she drove her single-seater Riley in a race at Brooklands, but the brilliance that had taken her to the top of the sport was no longer there, and it proved to be her last race.

The crash didn't seem to have affected her nerve, however, or her general zest for life, and she took up rally driving, starting the hard way by joining the Singer team as a navigator in order to learn the ropes. Kay became as popular with the rally competitors as she had been with the racing drivers and enjoyed the light-hearted antics that went on at the end of many events. On one occasion several of the men challenged the women to try their hand at 'parachuting', by jumping from the ballroom balcony of their hotel on to a heap of cushions on the dance floor below, using a large golf umbrella as a makeshift parachute. When nobody else would accept the challenge, Kay decided to have a go and it was probably only her light weight that enabled her to land safely, but whatever the reason nobody else was willing to follow her off the balcony.

Kay enjoyed the time she spent driving in international rallies and was particularly keen on the Alpine Rally, which she felt was always a test of courage and came as near to racing on public roads as it was possible to get, particularly during the high-speed timed sections, in which drivers had to keep to time over snow-covered Alpine passes with their hairpin bends and stark drops.

She became a successful motoring journalist, working for Kemsley Newspapers, and was the first woman member of the British Guild of Motoring Writers. It was in 1939, while covering the last Monte Carlo Rally before the war, that Kay nearly lost her life for the second time. She was covering the rally for the *Daily Sketch* with Major Reggie Empson and they were on their way to Digne to join some friends for dinner at the Ermitage Hotel, when their car was in a collision with a lorry at some notoriously dangerous crossroads. Reggie Empson was killed outright and Kay was injured and rushed to hospital. Fortunately, on this occasion she was not as badly hurt as the first reports of the accident seemed to indicate, but the accident and Reggie Empson's sad death were felt by all the competitors and the press.

There were occasions when being the only woman attending some of the motoring press functions needed a mixture of tact and discretion on Kay's part, but if she felt that her presence was likely to cause embarrassment she always disappeared at just the right moment.

A typical example was a visit to Canada by a group of motoring writers to road-test the new Austin A40. Their route was over the Rockies and, as the weather was particularly hot one morning, several of them decided to take a cooling dip in a quiet roadside lake and parked their cars along the water's edge. A lack of bathing costumes didn't seem to matter and nude bathing was the order of the day. Several who had been swimming in the nude were just coming out of the water when Kay arrived, but she quickly summed up the situation and drove on past and out of sight. There were some embarrassed faces among the journalists when they met Kay at the lunch stop, but she never let on who or what she had seen that morning.

For a while Kay was also the Austin Motor Company's colour consultant and was responsible for a refreshingly bright range of colours, which were a feature of their new models, at a time when colour didn't seem a major factor with some motor companies.

When Henry Petre, who had always been so supportive of everything she did, died in 1962 Kay returned for a while to her native Canada, but found it too cold and moved back to England in the mid 1960s. During the later years she lived alone in her London flat until her death on 10 August 1994, at the age of 91.

In 1996 she was the first woman to be honoured with a place in the Canadian Motorsport Hall of Fame, and when Dave Defries, who was still living in her home town of Toronto, was asked what memories he had of his famous aunt, he replied, 'She was certainly the firecracker in our family and there was always a sense of awe when you were around her.'

20

The End of an Era

For more than thirty years Brooklands had been the place where people went to have fun and to watch some of the most exciting motor racing in Europe. The usual large crowd flocked there for the 1939 August Bank Holiday meeting and they were looking forward to a good day's entertainment, despite the newspapers and the radio news bulletins, which had been full of foreboding and the talk of war.

It was a beautifully hot summer's day and, after a week of wet and blustery weather, the circuit was bathed in sunshine and there seemed every prospect of some very exciting racing. Many of the top drivers were there and the talk was more about who would be the winner of the Campbell Trophy, which was the main race of the afternoon, than it was about the threat of war.

The accident to Kay Petre, who had always been such a warm favourite at Brooklands, was still on many people's minds, but those who were there that hot summer day were not to know that they would also be witnessing the end of motor racing at Brooklands. Had they been told then that within a few months a large section of the famous circuit, once the envy of the world, would be torn up and that the site would be sold to an aircraft company for a paltry £300,000, they probably wouldn't have believed it. Neither would they have believed that Malcolm Campbell, their motor-racing hero, who had raced at Brooklands from 1908 until 1935, would be one of those who would seal its fate.

Sammy Davis summed up everybody's feelings at the time when he described news of the sale as 'like hearing an old friend being sentenced to death'.

The racing at Brooklands on that August Bank Holiday, however, was first-class and Raymond Mays in his ERA beat the colourful Prince Bira in his Maserati to win the Campbell Trophy. Billy Cotton, the popular dance-band leader, won a race in his ERA and bespectacled Bob Gerard, Percy Maclure and Wilkie Wilkinson all won races in their Rileys.

The impressive works V12 Lagondas, driven by Charles Brackenbury and Lord Selsdon, which two weeks previously had been placed third and fourth at Le Mans, roared across the finish in close company to take first and second places in their races, with the burly 'Brack' Brackenbury, who sported a large moustache and always drove bareheaded, wearing his familiar old sleeveless sweater, putting in the fastest lap at 127.7 m.p.h.

Dorothy Stanley-Turner was the last woman to win a race at the circuit, which had been the scene of so many famous successes for women drivers, when she finished ahead of a strong field in her supercharged MG Midget and attributed her success to a lucky white-elephant mascot given to her by an admirer just before the start.

Then as the shadows started to lengthen and the car parks

began to empty, George Baker, in his American built Graham-Page straight-eight made motor-racing history by winning the last race to take place at the famous circuit, snatching victory from B Burton and his impressive 3-litre Talbot by a fifth of a second. George and his father Alec had been regular competitors at Brooklands throughout the 1930s and had the unusual distinction of frequently racing there together.

A month later war was declared and for the next four years all activities at the Surrey track were clothed in secrecy as it became involved in vital war work. The sad demise of the Brooklands circuit after the war was a severe blow to motor racing, but particularly to women drivers, who had not only brought additional glamour and excitement to the sport, but had built up a strong following among motor-racing enthusiasts. Their courage, determination and skill had brought them international success, but sadly when peace came they were left with nowhere suitable for them to race.

There were other reasons for the disappearance of women drivers from the motor-racing scene after the war, the most important being the cultural changes that took place. Women were constantly being told by the government, women's organisations and even sections of the women's press that, as they were no longer needed to work in factories making munitions, or to serve in the forces and the nursing services, it was now their duty to marry, stay at home, look after their husbands and have children. Racing motor cars was no longer considered the right thing for a patriotic woman to do.

Apart from the loss of Brooklands, most of the other circuits were either derelict, or being used for other purposes. The motor racing that was taking place was mostly on wartime airfields, which had no adequate safety precautions by modern-day standards and were not really suitable circuits for racing cars travelling at high speeds, even more so when most of them were old models with questionable brakes and steering.

The tragic deaths of several experienced and well-liked racing drivers made race organisers even more unwilling to see women back on the track and the possibility of injury, or even the death of one of them, was a risk they didn't want to take. The death of a man was bad enough, but the public outcry that would almost certainly occur if the driver was a woman could seriously damage the future of the sport at a time when everyone concerned was trying hard to get it re-established.

Even without this understandable opposition to their racing, there was a lack of suitable cars for women to drive. With the exception of some 500cc models, powered mostly by JAP and 'double-knocker' Norton motor-cycle engines, it would be some time before the appearance of any postwar racing cars and even longer before they were made available to the public. The prewar cars being raced were all owned by men, who naturally wanted to drive them themselves.

The odds were again consequently heavily stacked against women becoming racing drivers, as they had been for many years before the war, but this time the reasons were not only different, but even more difficult to overcome.

Although women didn't have the opportunities to race and prove they had the courage and ability to do so successfully, they were able to take part in the international car rallies that were increasing rapidly in popularity and importance. As the first new models for five years began coming off the assembly lines in greater numbers, manufacturers wanted to demonstrate their performance and reliability and rallies provided an excellent opportunity for them to do so and also get valuable worldwide publicity.

Women were having a greater influence on the cars being

bought than ever before and most of the leading manufacturers ran works teams made up entirely of women drivers. Doing so gave them not only a better chance of individual and team successes, but also an opportunity to compete for the special awards that were available only to women. Many of the official works teams also included several of the top racing drivers, and being able to compete against them did at least give women drivers an opportunity to show that they were no back numbers in international events. Some of the successful private entrants were also women, and others, such as Pat Appleyard, the daughter of Sir William Lyons, the head of Jaguar, teamed up successfully with their husbands. During the 1950s Ian and Pat Appleyard became one of the most formidable husband-and-wife teams competing in international rallies, gaining several important successes at the wheel of their immaculate white Jaguars.

The most successful all-woman partnership was that of Stirling Moss's brilliant young sister Pat and Tommy and Bill Wisdom's attractive daughter Anne. Apart from winning the Coupe des Dames in almost every major international rally on several occasions, they became Womens European Rally Champions and were the first British drivers to win the very demanding and dangerous Liège–Rome–Liège Rally, driving a works 3-litre Austin Healey. Donald Healey referred to their outright win in this long, fast rally as one of the greatest of the many victories achieved by his cars. Their win was all the more remarkable, as Princess Margaret learned when she met them at that year's London Motor Show and congratulated them on their success, because Anne Wisdom suffered badly from car sickness during every rally.

Bouncy Sheila Van Damm, whose father owned the famous Windmill Theatre in London, was another outstanding rally driver. She won the Womens European Rally Championship with the petite Yorkshire housewife Anne Hall, but, unlike those of Pat Moss, many of her impressive list of international successes were obtained with different co-drivers. Sheila was also an amateur pilot and one of the few women to race cars successfully during the 1950s, when she partnered Peter Harper in a specially modified works Sunbeam Rapier to win the 1,600cc class in the Mille Miglia in Italy.

When the first Sunbeam Alpine was announced in March 1953, Sheila accompanied Stirling Moss and Leslie Johnson to the Jabbeke Highway in Belgium, with the intention of creating a new class world speed record with a specially modified Alpine, which had been fitted with a metal undershield to improve the streamlining. After Sheila had again shown her versatility by covering a flying kilometre (0.6 mile) at 120.125 m.p.h., it was decided to let that stand as the new record. Leslie Johnson then took the car to Montlhery and covered 111.20 miles in an hour and Stirling Moss did a couple of laps at 116 m.p.h.

The attractive Irish driver Rosemary Smith was 24 and a successful fashion consultant in Dublin when she joined the Rootes team and in 1962 drove a works Sunbeam Rapier with Rosemary Seers in the very demanding Tour de France, which started at Rouen on 15 September and did not finish at Rheims until 23 September. It was one of the toughest events in Europe and included seven circuit races, one of which was of two hours' duration, seven high-speed hill climbs and 5,000 kilometres (3,120 miles) of fast sections, which took place over normal roads.

Apart from being a member of the winning team, Rosemary won the women's prize and the special women's handicap award. Her success proved a slap in the eye for the French authorities, who had refused to accept her as a reserve driver for the Sunbeam team at the Le Mans 24-hour race on the grounds that 'a woman could not match men in that high-speed event'.

It was rather ironical that the Le Mans circuit was one of those used in the Tour de France, and Rosemary's brilliant drive there won her the special award, but the decision of the French authorities was again proof that, nearly twenty years after the war, women were still finding unreasonable barriers being placed in their way by bloody-minded officials.

Fortunately, the situation is now improving and more women are competing successfully in club and national events, although none have so far made the same impact, or had anything like the same measure of success at international level, that they did before the war.

When in 1999 the Royal Automobile Club commissioned Dr Judy Eaton, a leading psychologist, to find out why motor racing is still a sport being dominated by men, her extensive research showed that, contrary to the views held by some officials, there are no physical or psychological reasons why women could not become successful Grand Prix drivers. What is missing is a level playing field. Women need to be taken seriously and given the same amount of help and encouragement while still in their 'teens that many young men get. Helen Bashford the chairman of the rapidly growing British Womens Racing Drivers Club, feels that if that is done, a breakthrough will occur before long at international level, particularly as there is now such a strong women's movement in Britain.

Women are now successful fighter pilots, airline captains and even professional steeplechase jockeys, none of which seemed even remotely possible only a few years ago, so perhaps those fast women, who made such an impact on motor racing before the war and brought additional glamour and excitement to the sport at the highest level, won't be the last.